The Girl Who Never Was

A handwritten memoir

Kate Barrett

Koala Cove Press

Published by Koala Cove Press
email: koalacovepress@gmail.com

First published in Australia by Koala Cove Press 2019

Copyright © Kate Barrett 2019

Kate Barrett asserts the moral right to be identified as the author of this work. All rights reserved. No part of this publication may be reproduced, stored in a retrieval system, or transmitted, in any form or by any means, without the prior written permission of the copyright owner.

Cover design and photo © Kate Barrett

In order to preserve their anonymity, the names of many people in this book have been changed. Certain locations have also been given ficticious names.

ISBN: 978-0-9875965-9-8
(paperback)

For my family with love,
and in loving memory of Dad and Kevin.

Staring at the whitened page,
Potential here for fool or sage
To set down his own little piece
On life or death or golden fleece.
Striving with verse and untamed metre
To carve a dud or a world beater.
Cast for words as yet unsaid
Smite the heart that has never bled.
Trim and cut and re-arrange
These tumbling thoughts to others strange.

— First verse of untitled poem by A. Barrett

Author's Note

I'm sure I'm not alone in cherishing fond memories of sending and receiving handwritten letters, back in the days when such activities were still the done thing. Each one was different, written in a scrawl unique to the writer. I remember the pleasure of finding letters, sometimes long-awaited, when checking the mailbox. Even before I began reading the message, a connection between the sender and me was created, simply by recognising the handwriting. Although the advent of emails has made communication much simpler and quicker, even the most heartfelt electronic missive loses some of its emotional power when compared to the same words scribbled onto the paper of a traditional letter. (And I'm assuming no-one has yet discovered a way to infuse the delicate hint of a lover's favourite perfume into a romantic email?)

While typing the first draft of this memoir it felt like I was writing a letter to a far-away friend and sharing a very personal secret with them. This gave me the idea of making my story into a traditional handwritten letter of sorts, using my own writing rather than a computer-generated font. At first it seemed like just another of my crazy ideas — and I've had a few — so I rather reluctantly rejected it, as it didn't appear to make any sense.

After all, there must be a good reason why other authors haven't already done it. But the recurring echoes of a distressing incident which affected me very deeply made me change my mind and I decided to follow my heart rather than my head.

My father spent the final two years of his life in a nursing home, suffering from severe dementia. His short-term memory was virtually non-existent and his ability to recall longer-term memories was patchy and fluctuating. Despite this, for a while he still had occasional access to his large vocabulary and would enjoy playfully using obscure or unusual words in his sentences. At other times he was distressed when unable to remember even an everyday word he used to know well. Dad had always loved words and over the years wrote a number of poems and short stories. It felt all the more tragic then, when one day he handed me a piece of notepaper and asked if the letter he had been trying to write to a relative made any sense. As I had feared, it was almost completely indecipherable, with only a couple of actual words scattered throughout. After a lifetime of delighting in the richness of language and communication, Dad had lost the ability to write down even the simplest of greetings. This event was a painful reminder of just how much we take it for granted that we are able to communicate with each other, and how much is lost when suddenly we can't.

The first drafts of this memoir were typed on my computer, as it's much neater and easier to make numerous changes on a screen than it is on paper.

Handwriting a manuscript soon results in the page resembling a literary war zone as unsatisfactory sentences are scribbled out, new versions squeezed into tiny gaps, and paragraphs re-arranged. Luckily, by the time I had stretched my laptop's patience to the limit with umpteen drafts of my manuscript, I was ready to transcribe it onto paper with a pen.

Once I had removed the intermediary of the keyboard I felt more tangibly connected with what I was writing, physically forming the words and sentences rather than delegating the task to a computer. And as I had hoped it would, it felt as if I was penning a handwritten letter to my readers rather than just typing it out in some anonymous font.

So this resultant tome is the love child of a conventional book and an old-fashioned letter. Hopefully it has inherited some of the strengths of each — the book's capability of reaching a wide audience, while keeping the extra degree of personal connection found in a handwritten letter.

Warm regards,

Kate Barrett
8th January 2019

Chapter One

Eighteen years after I had given birth to my son I realised I was a man.
There had been many clues, some obvious and others merely hints, strewn along the path of my life but I simply hadn't gathered them up and made sense of them. Until now I had also been missing the pivotal piece of information that could have led me to the truth. Without it, all the clues had been seemingly meaningless, but now knowing that I was a transgender gay man, a lot of things that had puzzled me throughout my 47 years finally made sense.

Chapter Two

I was born in Perth, Western Australia in December 1961, the beginning of what would be a very hot summer for one of the most isolated capital cities on earth. Apparently my parents and I survived the scorching heat, because within six years our little family had grown to include another daughter, Sarah and a son, Justin. We had also moved into the wheatbelt, 355 kilometres (220 miles) east of Perth, where the first clues to my real identity would soon show themselves.

My parents had bought a vast tract of virgin bush which Dad would gradually clear and transform into a productive wheat farm. Although a harsh semi-arid landscape, with low rainfall and blisteringly hot summers, the area had its own unique beauty. The bush was made up of spindly trunked mallee trees and other eucalypts, while thin-leafed shrubs formed the under-storey. Spring was my favourite season, when the normally muted tints of the bush would be transformed into a patchwork of colours. Pink everlasting flowers carpeted the dirt while spider and donkey orchids shyly hid in the undergrowth, challenging eager flower-hunters to find them if they could. The shrubs covered themselves in impressive displays of fragile, tiny flowers. Later, the heat of summer days would release the oils in the gum trees, thickening the air with the distinctive smell of eucalypt, a scent which even now evokes nostalgic memories of the mallee country. The bush was also home to a multitude of different creatures, including echidnas, emus and kangaroos.

Our little community of farming families was scattered over a wide area, with kilometres rather than metres separating neighbours. Each farm covered thousands of hectares, with our approximately 1,500 hectares (3,700 acres) being one of the smaller ones. Every farm in the area had to supply its own electricity with generators and collect its own water, either from rain or by carting it from one of several locations. Mount Hannah was not even a dot on most maps and consisted of the primary school and a wheat bin.

At the time I began attending the school in year one, it consisted of an asbestos classroom with a tiny semi-enclosed verandah in front, approximately ten students of various ages, and a young male teacher. It had only recently been built and there were no lawns, gardens or school canteen. The oval and playgrounds were bare earth and our drinking water was kept cool in a hessian water bag hung from the verandah. The entire school grounds, which appeared vast to my five-year-old eyes, was surrounded by the natural bush out of which it had been claimed. The toilets, housed in two tiny corrugated iron sheds, were situated very close to the bush. For the first few months every visit to them was nerve-wracking, as I always half-expected to be greeted by some snake which had lost its way. Fortunately this never happened, but I was always aware and wary of the possibility of encountering one whenever playing or walking in the bush. Dugites and Tiger snakes were two deadly species which inhabited the area.

Due to the small number of children and the fact that we shared the same classroom and teacher no matter what year we were in, it wasn't long before I knew all of my fellow students. Most of them were very friendly and easy to get on with.

In many ways I enjoyed school and quickly discovered the joys of reading, as well as writing stories, both of which have proved to be enduring passions. My memory is not up to the challenge of recalling my first literary attempts, but I assume they were simply two or three sentences describing my latest childish pursuit or family event. A drawing illustrating the action would then have completed the exercise.

One piece of writing from my childhood does remain clearly etched into my memory, but this was certainly not done as part of a classroom assignment. I don't know exactly what age I was, but imagine it was somewhere between six and nine when, in a fit of desperation one night, I wrote a heartfelt plea to God. I remember placing the note, written in my best handwriting, on my cupboard just before climbing into bed. I was hoping that sometime during the night while I slept God would read my request and grant me my greatest wish. Within moments of waking the next morning my hopes were shattered, replaced by despair. He had not changed me into a boy during the night. Not wanting to give up, and hoping that perhaps God had been too busy to read or act on my request, I repeated the process for another few nights. Finally however, I accepted that no amount of pleading or wanting would change my reality. I was a girl and would be staying that way, no matter how emotionally painful it was.

   Luckily I realised, even at such a young age, that my desperation to be a boy wasn't information I should share with my fellow classmates. However, I did tell Sarah about it at the time, news that she presumably took in her stride. Although I didn't disclose my gender preference, and I didn't look like a boy, perhaps there was something about me that made me come across a little differently from the other children. I got on with most of my classmates, but there was one girl who picked me out as her victim, and bullied me on and off over the years we both attended the school. Being a charismatic personality, she also often enlisted one or two others to join in. Probably most of the school population felt the brunt of her emotional abuse at different times, but I and a couple of others seemed to be her pet projects. Until recently I had always assumed I had been victimised due to my extreme, almost pathological shyness. However, now I wonder if she unconsciously picked up on some difference in me, perhaps a faintly male energy. And because she couldn't cope with anything she didn't understand, she reacted according to her own personality, which was to be aggressive.

Going to a rural school with very few students meant it was harder to hide from my tormentor, but in other ways its small population was a benefit. It meant that we were taught all of the team sports, with no distinction made between boys' games and girls' games. This was because there weren't enough of each gender to play a proper game if the other were excluded. Thus, the boys learnt and played netball, and the girls learnt cricket and Australian rules football, as well as the mixed games like volleyball. I loved learning how to kick, handball and mark a football, which I would never have experienced in a larger school. This advantage only went so far however.

Occasionally we would all attend a sports carnival, where our teams competed against a number of other schools in the area. The girls played netball and the boys played football and if a school didn't have enough to make up a team it would combine with another. At these carnivals I would see the boys in their football jumpers and boots, all of them hopeful of muddy glory as they headed off to do battle, and desperately longed to be part of it. However, there was certainly no question of a girl playing football here.

I also very much wanted to own a pair of football boots. I would look on with a hopeless longing as some of the boys changed into their boots before heading into the playground to kick the ball about during recess or sports lessons. During play times the boys would usually stick together, while the girls went about their separate activities, although sometimes the two groups joined up for various games like "What's the time Mr Wolf?" or "All over, red rover," which required more participants.

    The small school population also provided the occasional cross-gender opportunity in other arenas. One evening in December each year, just before the long summer holidays, we would put on a school concert. This usually included singing a collection of songs as a whole-school group and a couple of plays. This was combined with Father Christmas arriving on the back of a Ute and giving out presents to all of the children. It was one of the area's major social events. Every student was included in the concert and for many weeks before the big night we would be learning our lines, rehearsing, and having our costumes sewn by our mums. One year, as a group of us were given copies of the script in order for an initial run-through of the story, I chose or was given one of the male roles to read aloud. I had no idea the characters we were reading out at that point were likely to be the parts we were given. There weren't enough boys to fill the male roles so when the teacher heard me confidently reading the lines, I was given it. At first I was horrified as it was one of the leading roles, which meant being on stage for almost the entire play. Being chronically shy, this was the very last thing I wanted. However, as the weeks passed and we learnt our lines and began rehearsals, this terror was mixed with the happiness of being able to openly play at being a male. When we began actual dress rehearsals I was even happier. On the day of the performance I felt sick with nerves, but once on the stage I began to enjoy myself.

Some parts of the school curriculum were very firmly segregated along gender lines. Once a week the boys would be taught manual arts, which mainly involved learning woodworking skills, while a local woman would come in to teach the girls needlework. Being the 1960's and 70's in rural Australia, this automatic division was unquestioned. Although I thought it was a pity that we didn't all learn everything, I really enjoyed the sewing lessons, so this exclusion from the boys' activities didn't bother me greatly. Mum filled the sewing teacher position for awhile and Sarah and I both enjoyed having her as our teacher.

At home I was free to play with whatever I wanted, without being restricted to "girl" toys. My interests were wide-ranging, and took no notice at all of gender stereotypes. I loved baking cakes and pastries alongside Mum and Sarah, as well as enjoying the various crafts we did. Although I owned and enjoyed playing with traditional female toys such as dolls and stuffed animals, I also liked more male oriented games and interests. One of my occasional hobbies was assembling and painting plastic model war planes and ships, my favourite being a Lancaster bomber which I spent many happy hours working on.

I was also a voracious reader, visually devouring virtually anything with words on. War and Phantom comics were two of my many favoured genres, but I also loved the more traditionally female oriented stories such as 'girls and their pony club' tales and English boarding school adventures featuring schoolgirls and their various exploits. For a few years my favourite reading choice was Enid Blyton's Famous Five book series, which featured four intrepid English children and their dog. I loved reading about their crime-solving adventures, and it was probably these early stories that kindled my life-long enjoyment of the mystery and crime genres. This series was my childhood favourite because, as well as the exciting tales, one of the girls in the group didn't like being one, and insisted on being called George rather than Georgina. She dressed like a boy and had her hair boyishly short. Obviously I could relate to her, and must have felt some reassurance to know I wasn't the only one who felt this way, even if George was only fictional. I remember that I wanted to be like one of the boys in the group, Julian.

For Christmas the year I turned eleven I was given a much longed for horse, a wonderfully gentle retired trotter named Mike who at 15.2 hands towered above me. When I rode him I would often imagine myself as a cowboy astride my black and brown heroic steed galloping across the American landscape, the paddocks of golden wheat transformed into vast prairies.

Sarah, Justin and I all had cap guns and would sometimes pretend we were in the Wild West, imitating scenes from the countless Westerns that were a television favourite at the time. During these games I would usually declare that I was a cowboy.

Although Sarah, like many country girls, was something of a tomboy, she never played any male roles and was always a cowgirl during these games of make-believe.

My siblings and I also played with armies of little green plastic soldiers, creating battlegrounds in the patches of sand near the house, or with small metal Matchbox vehicles (affectionately referred to as dinkies). At other times the three of us would happily wander through the bush, making rough cubby houses out of leafy branches. In later years I would ride an off-road motorbike along the dirt tracks which criss-crossed our farm and Dad taught us how to shoot a rifle at water-filled tin cans.

When I was in my early teens a fancy dress party was held in one of the nearby towns. I decided to go dressed as the Phantom, my favourite male comic book hero at the time. I enjoyed helping Mum to make my costume, and was very happy to be able to attend the party as a male character. Sarah was more conventional, choosing to go as Supergirl, and Justin went as a penguin. I was probably the only one who came as a member of the opposite gender.

Sometime in my early to mid teens, while browsing through the clothing section of a Perth department store, I discovered women's jeans for the first time. Although I couldn't get a pair that day, it was enough to know that they were out there. When jeans became popular as casual wear for both men and women in the 1970's I was overjoyed. Denim jeans were far less girly than slacks and I loved them. Although I preferred shorts and pants, throughout my childhood I had a few dresses and skirts which I loved. I was always excited when Mum was sewing me a new dress. I can't remember how comfortable I felt while actually wearing them, but I thought they were very pretty. And I still remember the excitement whenever Mum bought us new pyjamas, with Sarah's and my summer nighties being very frilly and flowery, which I know I did enjoy wearing.

I never cared whether a particular activity or interest was outside the norm for a girl to be doing it or not. I thought that being restricted to gender specific pursuits was senseless - and I still do. I didn't realise at the time how lucky I was that society was fairly tolerant of so-called tomboys. As society at that time regarded males as being the superior gender, it was considered logical that many girls would want to behave boyishly. In contrast, most of the girls trapped inside a boy's body, and who openly tried to explore their femininity would have met with severe hostility. Unfortunately, although the situation has improved a little since my childhood, this would still be the case for very many trans girls.

Chapter Three

My tormentor-in-chief left the Mount Hannah primary school before I did, so my last year there was spent blissfully bully-free. Quite a few other students also breathed a sigh of relief that they would be seeing no more of that particular girl. A new teacher also arrived at the beginning of my final year and the atmosphere of the school was changed markedly. Our new teacher, a young man with a lovely wife and two small daughters, was even-tempered and fair and motivated each student to do their best. We thought he was great. There were four of us in year seven and we all got on well together. That year was the most enjoyable of all my time at school, a brief interlude of relatively carefree childhood before we were to scatter to various high schools all too soon.

As the nearest secondary school was many kilometres away, with no bus service between there and Mount Hannah, most children from our area went to boarding school after finishing their primary schooling. Mum and Dad felt that at twelve years old I was too young to board. They were also worried that being so shy, I was bound to become the victim of bullying, a problem which was rife at the Wattle Rock student hostel. Wattle Rock was a town of approximately 3,000 people and the nearest with a senior high school, so Mum, Sarah, Justin and I moved there into a small three bedroom house. We made the one hour drive back to the farm every Friday afternoon to rejoin Dad, returning to town Sunday evenings. It wasn't an ideal situation, but Mum and Dad considered it the best option available for the time being.

    I began my high school experience with no self-confidence or assertion skills at all. The frontage of my new school grounds was impressive, with neat red brick buildings surrounded by deep-green lawns and well-stocked garden beds, but I was unable to appreciate any of this at the time. I was too overwhelmed by the size of the campus, which seemed to consist of a labyrinth of classrooms and a teeming horde of teenagers. Very different from the (by now) two classroom, thirty student school I had recently graduated from. Only one of my former classmates from Mount Hannah was attending Wattle Rock high school and we did not share any classes. Luckily I soon made friends with two of my new classmates, one of whom lived a few houses along my street.

    Perhaps inevitably, my excessive shyness marked me once again as the natural prey of the school bullies. My classes didn't always coincide with those of my two new friends and whenever I was not in their company I was frequently subjected to taunts and verbal abuse. This had the effect of drawing me even further into my fear and shyness.

    Our winter uniform was grey trousers or slacks and jumper, the jumpers being the same for both sexes. Surprisingly, considering this was in 1974, the girls had the choice of either wearing exactly the same style of male trousers as the boys did, or a specifically female style pant. (Slacks) Of course, I was delighted with this, and didn't hesitate in choosing the male style trousers. I was very happy the day Mum took me into the men's and boys' section of the small clothing shop in town and I was able to actually try on male clothing.

One incident of bullying may have occurred because I had chosen the male-style trousers as my winter wear. As I entered the girls' toilet block during a morning recess I saw that the small group gathered at the hand basins included a girl who was often unfriendly towards me. Ignoring the glare she fired at me I went into the nearest cubicle and closed the door. Seconds later she spoke, loudly enough that I could not fail to hear her.
"For a second when she came in I thought it was a boy invading our toilets. Easy mistake to make, don't you think?"
The others laughed appreciatively. I cried.
One reason I was very upset by the comment was because its sole purpose was to hurt me. It was also another blow to my confidence, because at that time I thought I was a girl, however unwillingly, and I wasn't sure if she had genuinely mistaken me for a boy or not. Even though I didn't want to be a female, because I was, I wanted to be seen as a normal girl.

Although school was an emotional endurance

. test, it was a novelty to live in a town where friends and shops were within walking distance. The simple act of going to the corner delicatessen to buy ice-creams or chocolate was something I had never done before. Wattle Rock was a small town with most of the shops fitting comfortably along one main street but to kids from a farm it was as exciting as living in a city. We still looked forward to Friday afternoons however, when we would pack up the car with belongings, food supplies and our poodle, Cinda, and drive the ninety seven kilometres (sixty miles) back to the farm. For me, school and all of its horrors seemed a long way off when Sarah, Justin and I were playing in the bush or riding our bikes along the dirt tracks.

The weekends never lasted long enough and Monday mornings always arrived before they were due. End of term and end of year holidays were coveted pockets of relaxation where for a few weeks I could re-enter the carefree state of mind I had enjoyed in the year before beginning high school. Now the time spent at the farm was even more treasured because of its fleeting nature.

Although I was probably unaware of it at the time, due to dealing with my own struggles, Mum and Dad were finding the domestic arrangements quite challenging. Early in my third year of high school it was decided that I would go to Perth, stay with relatives, and attend the nearby school. The rest of the family would return to the farm, with Sarah and Justin once again attending Mount Hannah primary school.

I don't really remember my feelings about this

plan prior to it being put into action, but I probably had mixed emotions. Presumably I would have been happy to be leaving Wattle Rock high school but nervous about the one I was about to go to. I certainly knew that I would miss my family, friends and the farm. I reluctantly sold my horse Mike, as I wouldn't be home enough and Dad was too busy to ride him regularly. No-one else in the family rode horses. I missed Mike intensely from the moment I watched him being driven away and hoped he would be happy in his new home.

Unknown to us at the time, the school I would be transferring to had the dubious reputation of being one of the roughest in Perth, an allegation I was soon to wholeheartedly believe. With 1,200 students it was also approximately twice the size of Wattle Rock high school, which was a challenge in itself.

My relatives were easy to get along with and provided me with a secure, safe environment, but they couldn't protect me during school hours. They had no idea what I went through at school, as I didn't tell them. I felt humiliated that I was being bullied, feeling that somehow it was due to my own inadequacy that I was being victimised. The seven month period spent in Perth that year was the most difficult time of my life up to that point. I was almost constantly targeted for abuse, including a physical attack which ended up in a blood nose. I returned home during term breaks but these times were overshadowed by the knowledge that I would soon be returning to Perth. I was desperately homesick between these brief respites, as well as severely depressed.

Chronic shyness and a fear of drawing any attention at all to myself made it virtually impossible to begin or continue a conversation with anyone I didn't know well. Any group situation also caused considerable anxiety. A few times when working in groups in class I would hesitantly put forward a suggestion or idea, and to my dismay be ignored. It was not until years later, when someone gently suggested that I try to speak more loudly because they could hardly hear me, that I realised my classmates hadn't been ignoring me, they simply hadn't heard me. Due to my fear of saying the wrong thing I had unwittingly made myself virtually invisible to those around me. Unfortunately this invisibility didn't protect me from my tormentors.

    Towards the middle of the final school term for the year an incident of bullying took an unexpected turn. I was trying to get access to a washbasin in the toilets, but three or four girls were deliberately blocking my way. Despite repeated timid requests for them to move they stood their ground, scornfully telling me to just go away. I felt a sudden surge of frustration and anger, fed-up with always being the object of their derision. Without warning, and to my surprise as much as theirs, I suddenly lashed out and hit the upper arm of the girl nearest to me. It was only a mild slap which wouldn't have hurt, but the completely unexpected nature of it caused her to step back from the basin with a look of total incredulity on her face. The others stood there with expressions of disbelief which probably matched mine. Immobilised with shock, I waited fearfully to see what the girl's reaction would be. To my relief, in a tone close to respect, she simply said, "She actually fights back," before turning away, telling the others to follow her and leaving without another word. To my considerable surprise this incident marked a complete change in these girls' attitudes. For the rest of the year they were friendly whenever we encountered each other and one of them even complimented me on a drawing I had done during an art lesson.

  That incident was not the only one to cause a major shift in attitude during those last weeks of the school year. This time however, it was me who experienced it. During one of our weekly lessons, on which subject I'm no longer even sure of, I suddenly saw the teacher in a different light. One moment I was only half-concentrating as he talked about some concept or other, the next I was seeing the person standing at the front of the classroom as a very physically attractive man. I had, for as long as I could remember, noticed whether I considered the males I saw good-looking or not, but this was a new and rather exciting emotion. Up until this point I had simply wanted to be a male, I hadn't actually felt a physical attraction to one. I had never been physically attracted to females either. Sexuality of any sort simply hadn't been on my radar. I had known that one day I would like to have a boyfriend and get married but it had all been academic, I hadn't actually felt it on a physical level.

  This experience altered my thinking considerably. For many years, once safely in bed for the night and inside the privacy of my own head, I had made up imaginary stories. This night-time daydreaming relaxed me and I would slip effortlessly into sleep. In these stories I would always be a teenage boy hanging out with other imaginary male teenage friends and basically living the life I so desperately wished I could have in reality. After the "awakening" incident at school however, these imaginary stories suddenly became complicated. Now that I was interested in boys my alter-ego wanted to date them, but after a few attempts in this direction realised this story-line didn't work. Although I knew about the existence of homosexuality, it was still illegal at that time (1976) and very socially unacceptable. It was never referred to by the teachers at school or in any of the books I read and rarely spoken of by anyone I knew - and never positively. I didn't have a moral issue with it, but because life was made so difficult for homosexuals and there was such a stigma attached to being one (or even being suspected of harbouring such inclinations), I didn't feel comfortable going down this path even in my imagination. I was dismayed to discover that my night-time alter-ego was no longer content to hang out with his male friends on a strictly platonic basis and I realised I would have to let him go.

My new awareness of males as future romantic partners caused a profound shift in my attitude about being a female. I now felt, for the first time in my life, that there was actually a positive aspect to my being a girl rather than a boy. It would actually make life easier once I began dating later on, I thought naively.

It was at this point that I pushed my intense desire to be a male deep into my sub-conscious, where it would stay, relatively quietly and unnoticed, for a few years. I did this because I knew, or thought I knew, that there was no way I could ever become male, no matter how much I longed to be, so I needed to somehow accept my femaleness. I was hopeful that I could do this now I felt there was a considerable future benefit if I could embrace my femininity. Not that there was any hurry to swap my jeans for dresses and skirts. Due to my socially crippling shyness I held no hopes of attracting any positive male attention at school. My romantic dreams reached further into the future.

    The school term finally ended in late November. The year ten students traditionally broke for the holidays a few weeks earlier than the younger grades, and I was back on the farm shortly before my fifteenth birthday. Mum and Dad had put the farm on the market some months earlier, deciding it was time for the whole family to return to Perth. Sarah was due to begin high school the following year and Justin two years later, so Mum and Dad felt it was simpler to be in the city rather than the country. It was a painful decision to make, as Dad had carved a productive farm out of the bush, clearing every paddock mostly by himself, but he and Mum both felt it was important to keep the family together. Perth also offered more educational and employment opportunities for my siblings and me.

    That final summer on the farm was filled with a mixture of emotions for all of us. Sarah, Justin and I had spent a large proportion of our lives there and it had been a wonderful and enriching experience. We knew we would miss it deeply. Every paddock, track, area of un-cleared bush and rocky outcrop was familiar and important to us.

The farm had been an ideal environment for us to grow up in. Many happy hours had been spent playing in the bush, making huts out of branches and leafy foliage, and forging long and winding trails. In effect, we had an enormous backyard, as the only areas out of bounds were those where Dad was currently working - clearing bush, ploughing, seeding or harvesting the wheat crop, depending on the season. Our bicycles had covered many miles as we sped along the gravel tracks which criss-crossed the property. This mode of transport was later supplemented by an old Austin A40 car which I learnt to drive at the age of ten, and an off-road motorbike.

I had also spent many blissful hours going on long gallops around the paddocks on Mike, enjoying the distinctive horsey smell as his muscles powered us to ever greater speed and freedom, me whooping with sheer exultation at the magic of it. Although Mike was content to walk, trot or canter as we headed away from home, once we turned around to come back, galloping was the only speed he had, and I didn't have much say in the matter.

Sometimes the whole family would take a packed lunchbasket into one of the many bush areas of the farm and enjoy a picnic and treasure hunt. A yearly ritual we all looked forward to was going on a Christmas tree hunt in mid-December. We would scour the bush for a perfectly shaped, perfectly sized pine tree. Dad would chop it down, load it onto the flat-bed truck and take it back to the house. We would then stand it up in a sand-filled bucket in pride of place in the lounge room. Mum would hang the various streamers and decorations around the room while Sarah, Justin and I were let loose on the tree with ornaments and lengths of different coloured tinsels. The result probably wouldn't have won any Best Dressed Christmas Tree contests, but to us it was perfect. The tree, seemingly holding no grudges at being cut down in its prime, would contribute further by filling the air with its gentle fragrance, a scent that even decades later often returns me to the magic of childhood Christmases.

    The country lifestyle was special but we knew that moving to Perth would give us the opportunity to sample a whole new set of experiences. Although I had already had a recent taste of Perth and it was a bitter one, I planned on finding a job when we moved and was optimistic that living there would be much better this time around.

    Once back in the city, and after some discussion with Mum and Dad, it was decided that rather than looking for work I would return to complete high school. By coincidence our new house in Perth was situated in the catchment area for the same high school I had been to the previous year. So I found myself back in the place I had recently thought I was saying goodbye to forever.

    Luckily the situation was very different this time as my tormentors of the previous year had all left school, having reached the minimum legal age to do so. Socially the conditions were much improved but I soon discovered that upper school was much more demanding academically than the lower years, requiring a level of study skills I didn't have. Up until this point I had done reasonably well in my school work but now struggled to keep up with the rest of the class. Two-thirds of the way through the year Mum and Dad reluctantly agreed to let me leave school and look for work. I left a few months before my sixteenth birthday, with minimal social skills and even less self-confidence. Although the final months spent at school had been quite pleasant, having made a few friends and not being harassed at all, I hadn't recovered from the damage that had been done during the previous years.

    Despite my shyness and insecurities, as well as the daunting prospect of now having to look for work, I was very excited at finally joining the adult world outside of school. I was hopeful that life would be easier now and that somehow I would be able to transform myself into a confident, outgoing young woman. Naively, I thought that by changing my life situation I would miraculously gain all of the social skills and confidence I needed. Of course life doesn't usually work this way but it would be a few years yet before I fully acknowledged such an inconvenient fact.

Chapter Four

Within days of leaving school I eagerly began looking for a job, energised by the prospect of entering the exciting world of work and earning my own money. Fortunately jobs were reasonably easy to get in 1977 so it was only a few weeks before I was offered the position of junior sales assistant in a central city luggage shop. Surprisingly, despite feeling stiff with nerves during interviews I can often get through them successfully, hiding behind a calm exterior while my emotions run amok within. This facade of confidence crumbled quickly and completely when faced with the demands of the actual job. My chronic shyness with strangers made dealing with customers quite an ordeal for me. It probably wasn't much fun for the hapless shoppers either. Belatedly realising that I was completely unsuited for the position, I resigned after four rather harrowing days. If I hadn't I'm sure I would have been dismissed anyway, as it was very obvious to the Manager and other sales staff that I was sinking rather than swimming.

Before embarking on my stellar four-day sales career, I had sat the entry test for clerical positions in state government departments. After sitting these tests everyone was ranked in order of results and offered jobs as they became available. In early November, a month before my sixteenth birthday, my turn came and I was offered a position with the

State Land Tax Department. Although the work was very repetitive and routine, most of it filing, my new colleagues and supervisors were a friendly, happy group and I soon settled in. The clerical work was much more suited to my personality as, apart from answering the occasional phone call, I didn't have to deal with the general public.

    I'm not sure how often my desire to be male, a longing which I had tried to banish, re-surfaced during these years. However, the following example is one I do remember, probably because it was such a strong feeling.

    As a child one of my favourite story genres had been war comics, early reading material which sparked my interest in the military. A family outing to an open day at the RAAF Pearce air force base when I was fifteen fuelled it even further. I loved everything about the day including looking up at the fighter jets in their hangars, awed into silence by the speed and power I knew lay dormant within their sleek metal bodies. It was great walking around the various pieces of military hardware and watching the aerial displays.

    Wandering around the areas of the base which had been opened to the public and seeing the men and women in their crisp air force uniforms, I knew I wanted to be one of them. However, without conscious thought, I had immediately imagined my future self as a male member of the RAAF, rather than a female one. I wondered what it would be like, living and working on base, but I was speculating from the men's viewpoint, not the women's. Obviously that was a hopeless ambition but I still wanted to be part of it, even though it could only ever be as a woman. By the time we were driving home that afternoon I was determined that I would join the air force as soon as I was old enough.

When I turned seventeen, the minimum entry age for the defence forces, I was still employed in my clerical position with the State Land Tax Department. I was still very keen to join the air force, but due to my shyness and lack of self-confidence I had put this ambition on hold, intending to apply sometime in the future. However, only weeks after turning seventeen a friend from high school told me she was applying to join. As she talked about what she had researched regarding the lifestyle, job options, etc. I decided to also apply immediately. We both submitted our applications and were soon told when and where to report for aptitude, psychological and medical testing.

The appointed day finally arrived and it was with a mixture of nerves and excitement that I began the rigorous testing process. Later that day I was told that I had passed every test - all that is - except one. I had been very short-sighted since childhood and had worn thick glasses from the age of eleven. Knowing the air force didn't require its recruits to have perfect vision, I hadn't been too concerned about this aspect of the testing process. However, to my bitter disappointment my eyesight was simply too bad and I was not accepted. Fortunately my friend passed and within a few weeks was heading towards the eastern states and the beginning of her new career. I was very pleased for her but it was terribly painful knowing I wasn't going too.

This episode made me look seriously at my own employment situation, as the air force was no longer the career opportunity I had expected it to be. I decided I definitely didn't want to remain in an entry-level clerical position for the rest of my working life. But because I had left school at fifteen, as far as a government job went this was exactly where I would remain unless I completed year twelve high school or its equivalent. After discussing it with Mum and Dad, who said they would support me financially for the year it would take to complete, I resigned from my job and enrolled in technical college to study for my high school certificate. Unfortunately my study skills hadn't improved since leaving school and I only managed to pass two of the four subjects I needed (five, if I had wanted to go to university). Disappointed and angry with myself for wasting the year career-wise I began to look for clerical work, as well as once again sitting various government and bank entry tests.

In contrast to the previous year at college 1980 was very difficult. While looking for work and attending unsuccessful interviews I became very disheartened. The severe depression which had disappeared upon leaving high school returned. This was largely due to being in a worse position, job-wise and financially, than I had been a year ago and having no idea what I really wanted to do with my life. I felt that applying for entry-level clerical jobs again in both the private and government sector was only a short-term solution.

While studying at technical college the previous year, my social skills had improved, but not by much. Whenever in a group I was virtually mute, not being able to begin or maintain a conversation and I still always felt on the outer - different and lacking in some fundamental way. During my study year I had been in two relationships, each lasting a few months. Both of these men were chauvinistic and overbearing but I endured their poor behaviour and attitudes through a misguided gratitude that at least someone was interested in me.

Despite my earlier naive hopes that life would somehow become much simpler when I left high school I now felt that I was lacking in even the basic tools which were required to engage with it successfully. There was a constant need and longing within me, a need for I knew not what. Now I realise it was self-acceptance and confidence I was desperate for, a feeling of belonging to the human race as an equal rather than as the somehow deficient person I considered myself to be. And even though I had attempted to come to terms with not being a boy, this was only partially successful. The longing to be male, and "knowing" that of course this was impossible, would resurface at various times, causing considerable emotional pain. It also confused me, as I couldn't understand why I wanted to be a boy so much.

Until my realisation that I was transgender, I used to assume that my teenage depression, feelings of alienation and worthlessness were due to having been bullied throughout most of my school years. I also assumed my severely low self-esteem was responsible for my difficulties in forming healthy romantic relationships.

Although I still think my school experience

played a big part, I now know it wasn't the only reason for my poor mental health. Despite having no idea at the time that I was transgender, trying to live as a girl when I wasn't one emotionally was messing me up psychologically. I suspect that deep down my sub-conscious knew I was trying to play a role I had been seriously mis-cast in, but it wasn't letting my conscious mind in on the secret. Even if it had let me know who I really was, I don't know if it would have helped or made me feel even worse, as I wouldn't have realistically been able to do anything about it.

    I eventually got a few months casual work at the State Energy Commission through an agency I had signed up with. As the final day of temporary employment came closer, I began to seriously consider the idea of travelling as a way of breaking out of the narrow confines of my life.

Chapter Five

For years I had been fascinated by the U.S.A. and was very keen to visit it, but no-one in my small circle of friends shared my enthusiasm for the idea. I knew I wouldn't be able to cope going alone to a foreign country so decided to explore Australia instead. I would begin by heading east across the Nullarbor Plain. I had saved a reasonable amount of money during my periods of employment and intended to stay in youth hostels and buy a 60-day bus pass, so felt it was very doable financially. I did have serious concerns about whether or not I would be able to cope emotionally on my own and far from home, but was determined to try it and see what happened. I wasn't sure whether my over-riding emotion was excitement or terror. I had no idea whether it would be the most wonderful adventure I had ever had or if I would be returning within a week, overwhelmed by the huge world outside my limited experience.

The day finally arrived, my bulging backpack stowed in the storage bay of the bus and we pulled out of the terminal. It was early afternoon, 20th October 1980, and what I hoped would be my life-changing adventure had begun.

It would be hard to exaggerate how extremely introverted the eighteen year old stepping onto that bus was. There were wallpapers noisier than me.

During my school years, being noticed had often meant being abused. Even after leaving that environment and the threat no longer existing, I was still afraid to attract any attention to myself in case it proved negative. I also felt that I had nothing to say which could possibly be of interest to anyone. Whenever someone I didn't know well attempted to have a conversation with me I felt that my every utterance exposed me as the deficient person I believed I was. Because I always tried to keep a low profile I drew inwards, living more inside the worlds provided by books, movies, television and my own imagination than by reality. I was only able to relate to other people in a very limited way.

It was therefore surprising to everyone I knew that I had decided to travel half-way around Australia on my own, as it appeared to be totally out of character.

A strange, wonderful and liberating transformation came over me almost as soon as the bus had left the terminal. The first indication I had that my reality had somehow shifted was in the ease with which I could chat to the middle-aged English woman sitting beside me. Later on in the journey I also found myself happily talking to other passengers during our refreshment stops at roadside cafes. Although still nervous, it was as if my subconscious had decided that now I was in a new environment where no-one knew me I could be whoever I wanted, and it was certainly not going to be a frightened introvert.

Days later, as the bus reached the outskirts of Adelaide I felt quite daunted by the prospect of being alone in a strange city. But once I got to the youth hostel and was booked in for a few nights it all felt more manageable.

Throughout my ten week trip I stayed in youth hostels which were situated in a wide variety of locations, ranging from capital cities to tiny country towns, as well as tropical islands on the Great Barrier Reef. Although open to all ages the hostels were mainly used by young people. Most hostels had same-sex dormitories and bathrooms, with communal kitchen and living areas. Their rates were very cheap, much less than any hotel, and were a great way to meet fellow travellers.

Many of my days and evenings were spent sightseeing and socialising with other hostellers and it was fascinating mixing with other young people from so many parts of the world. I was sometimes the only Australian staying in a hostel, with most being from Britain, Canada, the U.S.A. and Europe.

Every day brought some new experience and for virtually the first time in my life I hardly read a book. There was no need to when I was having my own adventures and living my own stories.

A few weeks into my journey, while in a pub with a couple of fellow hostellers, I decided to have an alcoholic drink rather than my usual soft drink. I had been a non-drinker up to this point so didn't know what to ask for. One of my companions suggested ouzo and Coke so I agreed to try that. The first tasted so good and gave me such a warm feeling that I soon had a second glass in front of me. By the time this was finished I felt very relaxed and comfortable within myself. I was also delighted to note that my constant feeling of insecurity and shyness, which although subdued lately was still there, had disappeared completely.

The alcohol also made everything feel slightly larger-than-life, the music sounded better and jokes and conversation seemed wittier. The Kinks' song Lola was playing on the jukebox, the unusual lyrics of which had to be explained to me, and while listening to it a second time I doubted I would ever hear better music. (The song Lola is about a transgender person but not surprisingly the vague resemblance to my own situation didn't even register as a flicker of recognition in my mind. My subconscious was still determined to keep its knowledge to itself.)

I was eager to have a third glass of this seemingly magical new potion but fortunately the guys I was with realised I was already affected by the first two and convinced me to change to straight soft drinks.

That evening marked the beginning of my habit of drinking alcohol whenever in social situations for the rest of my trip. I found that after a couple of drinks my confidence level would rise and I would become very outgoing, making me feel like a real part of the group for the first time in my life. Although since leaving home weeks earlier I had been able to interact with people in a more normal way, discovering the dis-inhibiting effects of alcohol made these interactions easy and much more enjoyable. Unfortunately life rarely gives us simple solutions which don't have a price tag attached and it would not be very long before I discovered the huge cost which came with this one.

. Rather than being a magical potion, alcohol would come to reveal itself as the poisoned chalice it so often can be.

My 60-day bus pass expired by the time I reached Cairns in Far North Queensland so after a couple of days relaxing in this picturesque tropical town I decided to return to Brisbane by train, stopping occasionally on the way. I arrived in Brisbane on Christmas Eve. The following day the wardens of the youth hostel, a very hospitable husband and wife team, hosted a wonderful Christmas lunch for the residents. We all enjoyed ourselves immensely and were very grateful for their kindness and generosity. What could have been a day of loneliness and homesickness for young people far from home and family became one of camaraderie and celebration. After a week in Brisbane I flew home, arriving in Perth late on New Year's Eve.

This 10 week trip I took as a teenager marked a pivotal point in my life. If I hadn't broken out of my limited, safe environment and taken on what was, for me, a considerable challenge, I would have remained cocooned within my shell of debilitating shyness indefinitely. I used to be surprised at just how much being in a new environment had enabled me to become more out-going than I had ever managed to be in my familiar surroundings. Now I realise it was because I was externally focussed, excitedly exploring new places and meeting new people, rather than looking inwards so much.

There was probably another factor as well. The following theory may be quite wrong, but it might help explain my sudden and noticeable personality shift. Perhaps the dynamics of the youth hostels I stayed in also played a part. Although I met some who had teamed up together as couples during their travels, mostly the people using the hostels related to each other principally as fellow travellers. Their genders weren't as relevant as is often the case in mixed social situations. Instead, we were all simply people far from home and exploring Australia, sharing information about different places we had visited or joining up to spend the day touring together. Often evenings would be group outings to the local pub or cafe.

    Even though I wasn't consciously aware at the time how all-encompassing my gender issues were, I now suspect they contributed significantly to my lack of confidence, low self-esteem and poor social skills. Therefore, when I found myself in a new and different environment where my gender was to all intents and purposes irrelevant, I could interact more easily. I didn't have to try to conform to any gender specific behaviours. And in Australia in 1980 the lines between the genders were still very clearly defined. I always felt very inept compared to other girls whenever anything specifically female oriented was expected of me. For example, I never felt confident preparing food for visitors or helping in other women's kitchens at social functions. And the thought of earning a little money through casual baby-sitting jobs, as many teenage girls did, terrified me.

    During my travels I was interacting with guys around my own age in a non-dating context and although I was very aware of the attractiveness level of my fellow hostellers I was not actively trying to gain their interest in any way other than casual friendship. While staying at the hostels I formed platonic friendships with a number of the guys and delighted in spending time with them. This was the first time I had had non-romantic male friends since primary school and to my considerable surprise I discovered that I was very comfortable in their company. I actually found it easier to begin chatting with them than with the girls in the hostels, a situation I would not have believed remotely possible prior to beginning this journey. This theory would also explain why life became difficult again when I returned to Perth, reverting to my primary identity of teenage girl, rather than fellow traveller.

Chapter Six

My happiness at being back home didn't last long. As soon as the excitement of seeing the family again and the comfort of a few good nights sleep in my own room wore off, I became restless. Registering for work at the Commonwealth Employment Service and looking at the boards filled with job vacancies made me feel as if my old life was closing in on me again. Already I could feel the old introverted "afraid of my own and everyone else's shadow" personality taking over and my recent adventures taking on an unreal quality. I was afraid that the socially capable aspect of myself would retreat back into hiding, unable to cope with the return to my familiar everyday environment.

In an attempt to avoid this fate I decided to return to Brisbane, with the intention of finding accommodation and employment there for a year. I had very little money left and no experience of living away from home apart from my recent trip. Unfortunately, being desperate not to lose myself again made me oblivious to the blatantly obvious drawbacks in my plan. Despite Mum and Dad trying to convince me to stay home and find a job in Perth, by mid-January, approximately two weeks after returning home, I was once again on a bus and headed to Brisbane.

Predictably, I soon discovered that trying to find cheap but decent accommodation while on a strict budget and obtaining employment in a new city was a considerable challenge – vastly different to being there on holiday. At first I stayed at the youth hostel and cheap hotels (there was a three consecutive night limit at the hostel) before booking into a long-stay hostel. There was no time limit there but I only intended to stay until I found a job and could afford my own place.

While on my initial holiday the previous year my drinking had been controlled and moderate, only having a couple of glasses in social situations with fellow hostellers. During my time in Brisbane this situation changed markedly. Faced with the challenges of trying to establish myself in a new environment I began to use alcohol as a way of temporarily reducing my fears and stresses. Functioning through an alcohol-induced haze made everything seem easier and more achievable. Of course in reality the opposite occurred, it is very difficult to find a job or do anything effectively while semi-intoxicated for much of the time. When I was staying at the youth hostel I would sometimes go out drinking with fellow residents in the evenings. Later, after moving into the long-stay hostel I continued this with the friends I made there. If no-one was available to join me I soon began going to pubs alone or buying bottles of spirits and decanting them into partially emptied Coke bottles. I would then sit drinking them in King George Square in front of the town hall.

Many mornings, sick and remorseful, I would determine not to drink but would at some point during the day succumb to the temptation of putting a thin veneer between myself and sober reality. Thus began a vicious cycle, my depression and increasing inability to cope with being completely sober made me drink more, which in turn made me more stressed and depressed.

Clearly I was having a melt-down because I had set myself too great a challenge, when I didn't have the emotional or social skills to meet it. Presumably it was because of these very low self-esteem and coping skills that my drinking habits became so self-destructive in such a surprisingly short space of time. What's not so clear to me, as I try to squint back through the misty memories of decades, is whether my desire to be a male rather than a female was registering at all on my conscious awareness during this time. Maybe it was, but perhaps I was too busy simply trying to function – and failing dramatically – to consciously worry about what gender I was. Whether I was thinking about it or not, I assume the gender issue was still contributing to my inability to cope, both then in Brisbane and later on.

After a very long two months I returned home, feeling utterly defeated and demoralised by my failure to temporarily establish myself in Brisbane. Fortunately, once back home I was able to stop drinking and after a few months of searching, found casual clerical work. My colleagues were easy enough to get along with but I found it difficult to interact with them. As I had feared might happen, I had reverted to my chronically shy personality. I missed the easy camaraderie and social contact with fellow hostellers that I had enjoyed in Brisbane. I conveniently ignored the fact that it had been a very difficult time in every other way. I felt confused and disappointed by my inability to function socially at any effective level while back home, when I could do so in a different environment. Although in Brisbane I had often been drinking, even when completely sober I was much more socially confident than when back in Perth. It was as if I had learnt the lines from my childhood and early youth - those of a complete introvert - so thoroughly that it remained the only script I remembered while on my familiar stage, Perth. Only by being somewhere completely outside my normal environment did I seem to be able to re-write my character. It was just a pity that this new personality needed some serious editing.

    Perth wasn't usually the excitement capital of the nation, but sometimes it came close. These were the times when the American fleet came to town. For a few days the normally unremarkable streets would be teeming with thousands of sailors, their accents and uniforms filling the air with a heady whiff of exotic climes and lifestyles. Of course, this was the very subjective opinion of a teenage girl. As the sailors were all males I'm guessing most of the local lads saw it from an entirely different angle.

    During one of these times, having just finished work for the day I was sitting in the Hay street pedestrian mall listening to a busker for a few minutes before I caught the bus home. Before long a young American sailor who had also been listening to the singing came up to me, introduced himself as Tom and asked if he could buy me a drink. After hesitating for a moment at this unexpected invitation I agreed. We went to one of the popular taverns nearby which was full to bursting with sailors and local girls. Tom found some of his friends, who made room for us at their table. Tom and his friends were all very polite and friendly and there was a wonderful spirit of camaraderie in the room. I thought how much fun it would be, being part of such a group, young men living, working, playing and seeing the world together. This seemed like an ideal lifestyle. Once again I was filled with a sadness that it was the type of life I could never hope to access, even if I had been an American. The closest I would ever get would be as a spectator, like I was that evening. Tom and I went out a few times while he was in port and one day he took me aboard his ship, an aircraft carrier, and gave me a guided tour. It was very interesting, but quite sobering, to see the cramped living quarters and heavy work-schedules the sailors had to endure. Despite that, I still felt an ache in my psyche that such a world – being a young man in a close-knit community of young men – was closed to me.

Chapter Seven

Being employed didn't ease my depression or calm the restlessness and discontent that I felt. The urge to travel again became stronger by the week and I saved as much of my wage as possible with the intention of going on a working holiday around Australia. It seemed I never let common sense get in the way of a bad idea.

My previous unsuccessful travel adventure - or misadventure - hadn't deterred me for long. The failure actually strengthened my desire to try again, and this time to get it right. Towards the end of August 1981 when my casual job contract ended I caught a plane to Darwin, intending to travel and work my way around Australia for a year. Although at this point I had never heard of the term "doing a geographical," I was once again doing just that. I was trying to escape my own dysfunctional personality, but inevitably it was as much a part of the luggage I took with me as my toothbrush.

I only spent a week in Darwin before flying to Cairns, Queensland. Despite it being the last days of winter, Darwin's weather was already hot and humid, and would only become more so as time passed, so I decided to move on. I had liked Cairns a lot when I stayed there briefly during my initial holiday the previous year. It was a picturesque, medium sized town, comfortably situated between low rainforest-covered mountains on one side and the ocean on the other. It also had a relaxed, laid-back atmosphere as if in constant holiday mood, not surprising in a town which was a magnet for tourists. Like Darwin, it was also set very firmly in the tropics, but in Cairns the weather was mild and dry at this time of year. It wouldn't be competing with Darwin's heat and humidity levels until the beginning of summer.

    Within a day or so of landing in Cairns I was booked into a guest house, old and run-down but clean and comfortable. It was built in the traditional Queenslander style, sitting high above the ground on tall stilts as a defence against any floods which may come its way. The weekly rates were cheap and included the use of a communal bathroom, a fully-equipped kitchen and a lounge room. Long-term residents were welcome. One of the problems during my earlier unsuccessful attempt at establishing myself in Brisbane had been a lack of stable accommodation for the first few weeks, which was very unsettling. Because of this I was very pleased to have found decent affordable accommodation almost as soon as I arrived in Cairns. I felt that I was already doing better this time around.

    Despite the promising start, during my four months in Cairns I would have some of the worst bouts of depression I had ever suffered until that time. Earlier in Darwin, I had begun drinking alcohol again after having stopped almost completely while back in Perth. During my time in Cairns most evenings would be spent in a hotel bar, usually with one or two fellow residents from the guest house. When drunk I would become very outgoing, happy and full of energy. Those who only saw me in this condition would never have guessed that I was actually very shy and, for much of the time, also severely depressed underneath the facade. My happy, extroverted and at times reckless behaviour convinced my new circle of friends and acquaintances that I was just out to have fun and didn't really give a thought to the future or responsibility. In fact, I did care very deeply about how far off track I had drifted but didn't know how to go about changing course. It was as if I could only ever be pathologically quiet and shy or swing to the other extreme, becoming quite reckless and irresponsible.

At times my excessive drinking put me into potentially dangerous situations, and it was due to good luck rather than good management that I never came to any serious harm.

Often, if I had met up with friends or acquaintances at a pub earlier in the evening, I would walk home alone through the almost deserted late-night city streets. I was aware that I was vulnerable doing this, but my high alcohol-to-common sense ratio kept me confident that I would get home safely. Luckily I did always get back okay, but there were a few close-calls. One of the most frightening of these happened not in Cairns, but Brisbane when, sometime in late November, I caught the train and stayed in the youth hostel there for a few days. One evening a few of my fellow hostellers and I went nightclubbing in the centre of the city. Hours later, when the others left to catch the last bus back to the youth hostel, I decided to stay for awhile longer, presumably too drunk to be concerned about how I would eventually get home. When I eventually staggered out of the club, somewhere in the wee hours of the morning, I realised I didn't have enough money for a taxi. I decided to go and wait it out in St. George's Square until the buses started running again in a few hours time. The square was well-lit and open, with the occasional police foot-patrol going through, so I was optimistic that it would be fairly safe. I found a bench to sit on, and hoped I wouldn't sober up too soon. As I sat there, the occasional late-night reveller wandered past, often calling out a friendly greeting as they went on their way, or stopping to chat for a couple of minutes. I was beginning to think the time might pass more quickly and easily than I had feared, when a guy around my age came over and sat down next to me. He was very drunk and in high spirits, and asked me if I would come back to his hotel room with him, so we could party. I politely refused, saying I had already had enough partying and was just waiting for a bus. Undaunted, he leapt to his feet and grabbed my arm, pulling me up from the seat, laughingly telling me he was going to take me back to his hotel anyway. I tried to jerk my arm away, telling him to let me go, but he was too strong, and began pulling me along with him. At first I had assumed he was simply joking around, and would let me go, but when I realised he was seriously trying to take me with him, I was terrified. I wasn't able to fight him off and I couldn't see anyone else around who might have been able to help me. Despite my struggles, I was pulled relentlessly towards the edge of the square, the guy still treating the whole thing as a joke, laughing and pleased with the challenge of getting me to his hotel. As we got onto the footpath, I saw a lamppost a little further on. As we passed it I wrapped my free arm around the post and clung onto it as hard as I could. After unsuccessfully attempting to loosen my desperate grip on the post by pulling on my other arm, the guy let go of me while he reassessed his strategy. At that moment I saw a police car heading up the road towards us. I quickly raised my freed arm and frantically waved at them, hoping that they would see me and also realise I was signalling for help. Luckily they did see me and pulled up alongside. The guy had seen the police car stopping and had quickly staggered off, suddenly content to return to his hotel room alone. Perhaps the seriousness of what he was doing had finally registered on his alcohol soaked brain. Emotional with relief and gratitude, I told the police officers what had happened, and that they had saved me from being kidnapped. After they had calmed me down, assuring me I was now safe, they said they were just about to have a refreshment break at a nearby all-night cafe and they would buy me a coffee. They would then drive me back to the youth hostel to make sure I got home safely. Although this close call frightened me, unfortunately it didn't scare me away from drinking too much and getting into vulnerable situations again in the future.

Sometimes I was at the most risk of physical harm from myself. One night a session of drunken roller-skating down Cairns streets ended in me falling over backwards and hitting my head on the concrete footpath. If my shoulders hadn't taken the brunt of the fall first, before my head, I probably wouldn't have gotten back up. Another night, alcohol overcoming my terror of heights, a friend and I climbed out of a first-floor window and ran along the verandah roof-tops of the old buildings in one of the main streets.

My excessive, dysfunctional behaviour during this time was due to my having no idea how to function normally in everyday life. Each time I got a job my personality would all but disappear, so, desperate not to be invisible again, I was now overcompensating. I reverted to my old ways by indulging in a lifestyle of partying and "out there" behaviour. This was accepted and even encouraged by the people I was mixing with. I wasn't happy to be living this way and desperately wanted to be able to have a normal life. As time passed, my confidence in my ability to cope with any sort of steady employment completely disappeared. I felt like a total misfit, once again on the fringes of normal life but now for very different reasons. I was relying on unemployment benefits for income and the prospect of being on welfare indefinitely if I couldn't get my life together was terrifying.

During the four months spent in Cairns I only managed to find one job. This was working in a hot-dog stand at the annual 'Fun in the Sun' festival. The work was easy and fun but unfortunately only lasted one week before the fair moved on.

One Saturday evening, sitting on the post office steps waiting for a few friends to join me in going to the pub, I casually watched people walk by on their way to various venues. As a young couple strolled past hand in hand, well-dressed and perhaps headed to a good restaurant, I felt an almost crippling surge of loneliness and emotional pain, wondering if I would ever be a fully functioning part of normal society. Desperately afraid that perhaps I would never be able to pull myself out of the situation I had created.

I still assumed that my initial problems of low self-esteem and feelings of alienation had been triggered by being bullied at school and my recent behaviour had simply exacerbated them. Having this supposedly obvious reason to explain my problems stopped me trying to look any further for causes. Perhaps if I had, I may have stumbled onto the depth and significance of my gender issues and realised they were also a possible contributing factor. But then again, I may have missed the clues completely and remained totally oblivious despite the search.

These months in Cairns were by no means completely unpleasant. I had many good times too, and have a deep affection for the town and its surrounds.

Two of my most positive experiences remain clearly etched in my memory.

One weekend two English guys around my age who were also staying at the guest house joined me on the ferry to Green Island, a popular destination just off the coast. We spent the day walking through the bush, swimming and snorkelling in the coral and fish filled waters, and lazing on the crushed-coral beach. The beauty of our surroundings filled me with a joy and total peace which I had not felt for a very long time. The depression, which to a greater or lesser degree usually pervaded every moment, completely disappeared while on the island.

On another occasion, a friend and I spent the day travelling around the Atherton Tablelands in his small open-topped car. We walked through different parts of the rain forest for hours, delighting in the lushness of trees, palms and undergrowth, small streams swirling over the rocks and extravagantly coloured butterflies darting around us. Again, the richness of nature was enough to totally engage the senses so that everyday concerns were forgotten. My companions on these trips all agreed that they too had felt the intrinsic power and calm of our natural surroundings. Even at the time, I felt these days would remain with me for life. I had gained so much from these outings because I had been living in the moment, not the past or the future. I had also stopped being so introspective, and instead was looking out at the world rather than looking inwards. I had actually connected fully with life rather than distorting it with alcohol, anxieties or depression.

As the months went by my despair deepened until, very reluctantly, I decided it was time to go home. I had finally realised that my situation wasn't going to magically and spontaneously improve. If my life was to ever be on track I would actually have to take the necessary steps to get it there, rather than vaguely hoping that one day everything would be okay. As I said my goodbyes to the friends I had made, and boarded the bus for Brisbane, I felt sad about leaving Cairns and hoped I wasn't seeing it for the last time.

Christmas was spent at the Brisbane youth hostel, where once again the warden and his wife generously hosted a lavish lunch for all of the hostellers. After a week in Brisbane I flew home on New Year's Day 1982, twenty years old and with no idea how to cope with my life or the future. I was very disheartened by the knowledge that it was a year ago that I had flown home from my initial triumphant holiday adventure, when I had believed I had learned to deal successfully with a newly exciting world. Now, I felt that I had actually gone backwards since that time, even less capable of functioning than before my first trip because now I was using alcohol as a crutch. Although I didn't know it while sitting on the plane feeling sorry for myself, I had actually grown considerably in some ways. There were many positives to come out of the year I was currently writing off as a total failure.

Chapter Eight

Within days of returning home I once again registered for work at the local employment office, where I was told about a local government funded support group for unemployed youth. This group ran various general and employment-specific skills courses as well as providing support and advice on looking for jobs. I began to drop into the support centre a few times a week and soon got to know some of the other regulars. It wasn't long before people began inviting me to parties and other social events, which helped to lessen my depression and feelings of isolation. I was very happy to discover that I didn't revert back to my extreme level of shyness. Although not as extroverted as I had been in Cairns, I was able to interact with others in a normal healthy way — while completely sober.

I'm not sure why my pathological shyness didn't swoop down on me as soon as I returned home this time, as it had gleefully done in the past. Perhaps those four months in Cairns had been long enough to allow deep-seated changes in my ability to interact more effectively with others. Added to the previous two stints away from home, maybe I had now gained enough experience in being more extroverted to keep it going wherever I was. It was no longer entirely situational.

Once again I had my drinking under control, only indulging moderately at parties and other appropriate social gatherings. Because I didn't want Mum and Dad to know about my drinking I was careful to keep it in moderation. My drinking habit was apparently not too entrenched at this stage and I could still control it when the situation demanded it. In Cairns, and earlier in Brisbane, the stresses of trying to establish myself in environments far from home and family had been too overwhelming. Because of this I had found it impossible to avoid the lure of alcohol, but now back in Perth my life seemed reasonably manageable even while sober.

Although I was looking for employment, I had no confidence at all in my ability to actually keep a job if offered one, so much had happened since I was last employed. One of the courses offered at the support centre was St John's First Aid, which ran over a number of days. I enrolled and enjoyed the mixture of practical and theoretical lessons. On the final day of the course everyone was tested. We had to demonstrate that we had learnt enough to get our certificates, and to our relief we all passed. This seemingly minor exercise made a huge difference to my confidence. After being out of work and generally very dysfunctional for so long, the certificate represented much more than passing a short course. It showed me that I was still capable of functioning in a positive way after all.

Some time shortly after this I was reading

through the day's newspaper when an article caught my attention. Apparently there would be a primary school teacher shortage in three year's time and the education department was encouraging people to become qualified in this area. Although never having considered teaching as a career option it suddenly seemed a great idea and I decided to apply to the appropriate institution. Because I hadn't passed enough high school subjects, I needed to sit the Mature Age Entry Test which was administered by the College of Advanced Education. The college ran the three year teaching course I was hoping to get into. I was very excited when told I had passed the test and been accepted into the course which was to start in February, approximately six months away. Although nervous about my ability to cope with the demands of tertiary education, I now had a goal and felt more optimistic about the future than I had done for a long time. Not long after this I was offered a casual part-time position in a printing factory, where I worked until just before starting college.

Chapter Nine

The three years spent at teacher's college were to be among the best of my life. Those years also gave me the breathing space between the past and the future that I needed. It took a few weeks to settle into the routine of studying, writing essays and attending classes, but I loved the academic environment. My enjoyment of everything about this new venture was increased because it was such a welcome contrast from my recent experiences — an oasis of calm and normality. The campus was small and had a relaxed atmosphere, with the lecturers being very approachable and helpful. The vast majority of my fellow students were female, mostly seventeen year-old school leavers but with ages ranging through to the early fifties. I had turned twenty-one a few months before I started college.

Although quiet and reserved in class, I was still able to maintain the level of social skills I had held onto the previous year. My time in Queensland had had its positive side after all. I had now managed to find a comfortable middle-ground between the pathological shyness of my childhood and the wild extroverted behaviour of my travels. I made new friends and often went to the cinema, pubs and various events with them. I also kept in regular contact with friends from the previous year, going to their parties and generally catching up. For the first time I felt as if I had a normal lifestyle - socialising easily, having the occasional boyfriend and working towards my future. After a series of driving lessons I also got my driver's licence and bought a cheap car. Until then, I hadn't had the confidence to learn how to drive.

    Although I was doing my best to be like my peers, getting dressed up and putting on make-up to go night-clubbing, going on dates, etc. I still wasn't comfortable with my femaleness. Often when I was getting ready for a night out on the town, applying make-up and generally trying to "pretty myself up," my thoughts would stray to wondering what all the guys getting ready to go out were doing. I imagined them shaving, splashing on after-shave and making their clothing choices for the evening's adventures. The scenes which were conjured up always felt a bit exotic, the mundane actions transformed into some mysterious ritual. I wished I could swap places with them, but since I wasn't sexually attracted to females at all, I wouldn't have been interested in spending the evening chasing girls, as most of them would have been.

    I can't remember how often my gender issue came to the forefront of my thinking during these years, but I suspect that sometimes it was just a general background noise, barely registering on my consciousness. I always felt different in some way to other girls, but had put it down to my shyness and general lack of confidence. At other times though, the issue was determined to get my full attention. In my second year at college I joined a health club and attended regular aerobics classes. I also did sessions on various gym equipment designed to improve muscle toning and strength. During my times in the gym I would often look at the sculpted bodies of the males who were enthusiastically increasing their muscle mass. As well as admiring their appearance I felt desolated that I couldn't sculpt my body as they were. I was sure that I would feel much more comfortable and at ease if I could only go through life in a male body rather than the female one I had been given.

The course workload was quite heavy and many of the assignments challenging, but I managed to cope with it and got reasonable marks. At the end of the first semester when a lot of assessments became due at once, as well as exams being imminent, my stress levels rose enormously. I felt that my whole future hung on passing my subjects. Fortunately, I remembered that the psychology unit lecturer, Irene, had mentioned in class that relaxation techniques were very effective in reducing stress. I was excited that there were actually specific ways to deal with stress, as I had never heard of such a concept before. I asked her if she could recommend any books or courses on the subject, and to my surprise she offered to teach me some useful strategies herself. I gladly accepted. Using the techniques I managed to control my anxiety well enough to complete the assessments and pass the exams. Irene's help quite probably made the difference between passing and failing the semester. I had worked myself up into such a heightened level of anxiety that it had been difficult to concentrate on my studies. I don't like to even imagine what direction my life may have taken if I had left college at that point, and I will always be grateful to Irene that I didn't have to find out. She continued to help me with various issues and over time became a valued friend and mentor.

    I really enjoyed the actual act of teaching during my practical sessions in classrooms, as well as creating the props and aids used to explain various points. I got a lot of satisfaction in helping a child learn something new. However, there were other aspects to the role which I didn't feel at all comfortable with. Some of the classes I taught during my teaching practices included very disruptive children and I felt that I wasn't very effective in dealing with them, which eroded my confidence somewhat. Another difficulty was talking to the parents, although luckily during training this didn't happen often. Because of my time in Queensland I was still very unsure of what my real personality was. But I did know I didn't feel like the competent professional that parents and head teachers would expect me to be once I graduated. I also had serious doubts as to whether I would be an effective and inspirational teacher, and I knew from my own early school days how important this was. Because of these factors I decided sometime during my third year that I didn't want to be a teacher, although I would still complete the course and graduate.

    As our course progressed, my fellow classmates'

confidence grew. Most of the people I shared school placements with during our practical teaching periods seemed at ease and professional when interacting with the experienced teachers in school staff rooms. I felt different somehow, and couldn't imagine myself ever being like the self-assured and competent female teachers who filled the staff-rooms. Now I'm not surprised I had trouble picturing myself as a confident female teacher when I wasn't emotionally a woman. At the time, being oblivious to this minor detail, I assumed it was simply due to a continuing lack of confidence and self-esteem.

Tellingly, my most enjoyable teaching placement was in a class with a male teacher. Although I had previously been assigned to a number of other classes with lovely female teachers who were just as friendly and supportive, I had felt more relaxed with him. Presumably this was because I was not wondering how I could ever be like him in the future, and fearing that I would fail to measure up, as I had been with the women. Perhaps once I actually had my own class everything would have fallen into place, but then again perhaps not.

Although no longer wanting to teach, I had no regrets about having gone to college as I had begun to live a normal life. Learning how to live in an emotionally healthy way was invaluable and having this new skill was due to those three years.

Chapter Ten

Within a few months of leaving college I was offered a permanent clerical position with the State Energy Commission, where I had worked on a casual basis years earlier.

Mum and Dad had instilled in my sister, brother and me the importance of buying our own homes as soon as possible to ensure financial security. Sarah had already bought a two-bedroom apartment a couple of years previously and I was keen to follow her example. Soon after starting work I bought an old, partly renovated two-bedroom plus sleep-out brick veneer house from Mum and Dad. They had bought it the year before as an investment property. It was on a duplex sized block which was suitable for sub-division, so I bought the front half of the property which included the house, while they kept the back half. Sarah later bought the rear portion off Mum and Dad and built a new house on it.

Hard to believe now, with local house prices in the many hundreds of thousands, that it only cost me $30,000. It was 1986 and only a couple of years later Perth would experience a major housing boom, making it much harder for people to buy their own home. Unfortunately, the situation is even more difficult today, with many young people finding it virtually impossible to get a toehold on the housing market.

My job at the energy commission was very repetitive with a lot of filing and photocopying. At times there was nothing at all to do, so I was often bored rigid. The atmosphere in the office was relaxed, with a lot of light-hearted banter and joking around which was fun, but the actual work soon became frustrating. I was one of only four women in my section of the office and I thoroughly enjoyed being in a mostly male environment. A group of us would often go out to the pub for dinner and drinks after work on Fridays.

I still felt a strong desire for a challenging job and although I wasn't sure exactly what I wanted, my interests leaned towards working in a people-oriented area. After eighteen months I resigned and registered for casual relief teaching with a number of local primary schools. I reasoned that relief work would involve the aspects of teaching that I enjoyed - presenting the lessons and helping the children with their work - while avoiding many of the areas I wasn't confident with. While on-call for the casual positions, I looked around for any other work which might prove suitable. I eventually applied for a position as a live-in house-mistress at a boarding school in a small country town. The job involved supervising the female high school students outside of school hours. My interview was successful and a couple of weeks later I began my new adventure.

At times it felt like being caught up in an Australian version of the English boarding school novels I had read as a child. This story had it all - humour, tragedy and drama.

The girls were a decent bunch, and I was pleasantly surprised to find that I could relate to them fairly easily. Ironically, as an adult, I felt more comfortable with teenagers than when I had been one myself. Of course, I was no longer being bullied by them, I had more self-confidence, and was more out-going than I had been as a teenager, which made all the difference. And although some may have registered that I was different in some indefinable way, it wouldn't have mattered to them in the same way it would have done if I was one of their peers.

Despite all this, it wasn't long before I became restless again and felt that I wasn't really emotionally suited for this type of work. Although enjoying many aspects of the job, I found much of it very stressful. I left the school after two terms and returned to Perth for a few weeks before heading down south to the coastal town of Albany. Obviously I wasn't yet finished with doing geographicals. I was still trying to find my place in the world, not able to discover where I could fit comfortably into it. I still hadn't realised that this wasn't likely to happen until I could feel comfortable within myself, or why I was apparently unable to do so.

During my college years I had kept my alcohol intake to a healthy level, only drinking occasionally, socially and moderately. In the three years since leaving college however, the excessive drinking which I had thought was well behind me had become a problem once again.

During my time at the energy commission and the boarding school a lot of my socialising consisted of going to the pub with a group of friends and getting very drunk. Due to work constraints these occasions usually only happened once or twice a week, but in Albany my unemployment gave me far too much free time and my drinking increased considerably. Since having decided that teaching was not for me, I had been unsure about which direction to head in career-wise. Without any conscious intention to do so, I had slipped back into using alcohol as an emotional bandage. My drinking had once again become excessive, but it was in Albany that it finally got too serious to ignore. Not only was I drinking too often, but I was also bingeing to dangerous levels.

During my four months in Albany I did two weeks work experience on the local newspaper. I had organised the placement because I was interested in journalism as a possible career. But even though enjoying every minute of my fortnight there, I soon realised the strict deadlines would be too stressful.

Not being able to handle stress seemed to be a common theme in my life.

One of my tasks while working at the newspaper was to look through past editions from the archives and copy out any interesting articles which could be used as flashbacks. For a couple of days, in-between various other activities, I spent a lot of time reading copies from the 1960's and 70's, finding the occasional titbit and reminiscing with colleagues about the various television programs of those times.

After the newspaper office closed on the Friday of my second week, most of the staff adjourned to the nearby pub for drinks, an event I was naturally very happy to attend. Many hours later, shortly before closing time, those of us remaining said our goodbyes and headed off to our various homes. The house I shared with a guy and girl was within walking distance and I began my erratic journey in its general direction. As I weaved my way along the footpaths, passing various shops and commercial buildings, I suddenly thought how strange it was that everything in 1969 looked the same as it did in 1988. For some reason (probably a solid night on the booze), I believed the year was 1969. As soon as I "realised" I had travelled backwards in time, I was fascinated by how little everything had changed in two decades. Approaching a parked car, a relatively new blue sedan, my fascination turned to confusion as I tried to work out how a car that wasn't made until the 1980's could have suddenly appeared in 1969.

I didn't "return" to 1988 until I woke up the next morning hung-over and, when the memories came back, very concerned about my internal time travel experience. Never having heard of anyone hallucinating while drunk, I freaked out that perhaps I had caused myself permanent brain damage due to the excessive amount of alcohol I had consumed. My two house-mates, when told what had happened, laughed it off and assured me that I still seemed to be behaving as normally as usual.

This was only one of a number of incidents which happened after heavy drinking sessions in Albany and I sank into a deep depression, frustrated and angry that I had messed up my life yet again.

Luckily help was on its way, in the form of a man named Vic, who was introduced to me by an acquaintance concerned about my drinking. Vic had been a problem drinker in the past but had dealt with his addiction and now helped others with their alcohol issues. It took him a couple of months to convince me that I needed professional help, but eventually, after a number of drinking misadventures and worsening depression, I reluctantly agreed. Vic knew the staff at an alcohol rehabilitation centre in Rockingham, a coastal town just south of Perth, and strongly recommended that I book in for their three month residential course. At first I was very resistant to this, feeling that I would be able to sort myself out, given time. My parents had no idea that I had a drinking problem, either then or in the past. I had carefully hidden it from them, not wanting to cause worry and through being ashamed of my behaviour. Obviously, if I was to live in a rehabilitation centre for three months I would have to tell them about it, which I was very reluctant to do.

Finally though, when I admitted to myself that I needed professional help, I broke the news to them. They were very distressed but also very supportive and agreed that going to Rockingham was a good idea. Days later, Vic drove me to the rehabilitation centre and saw me safely booked in before he returned to Albany.

I had no idea what to expect and it was a relief to find a friendly and supportive environment at the centre. The room I was to share with another woman about my age was bright, comfortably furnished and spacious. The women were housed in a separate building to the men, with their own bathroom and living areas. Meals were prepared by a professional cook and served in the large communal dining room. The majority of the residents were male, with only three other women there when I arrived, the ages ranging from early twenties to mid-seventies. The staff who ran the centre were all reformed drinkers and very understanding, while at the same time maintaining a tight regime. If anyone returned to the centre drunk, or even having had one drink, they were evicted, with a set period before being allowed to return. For some of the residents the stakes were high, as they had been ordered by a magistrate to complete the thirteen week program. Failure to do so for whatever reason meant a return to Court and re-sentencing.

During my stay at the centre I finally realised that I couldn't afford to drink at all, or at least not during periods of my life when I was feeling lost and depressed. It had been a valuable experience to sit in group meetings and hear the stories of those whose lives had been destroyed by alcohol. Some still in their twenties had personal histories as filled with loss and regret as many of those in their sixties and seventies, and I was very aware that I had survived relatively unscathed in comparison.

The three months spent at the centre were very emotionally confronting, but it wasn't all work. Occasionally a group of the men and I would go down to the beach which was a short walk away and kick a football around. This was the first time I'd had a chance to do this since my teens, when Sarah, Justin and I would take a football down to our local park. I loved being part of a group of men, playing a predominantly male sport.

I have always enjoyed the company of both males and females and like having friends of both sexes. Most of the time I have had more successful relationships with men when it is on a "friendship only" basis, rather than in romantic situations. In a platonic friendship the gender make-up of the participants is relatively unimportant, but in a romantic relationship it is obviously the overriding consideration.

After leaving the centre I returned to Perth. My house was being rented by a young couple so I moved in with Sarah, who had recently bought the half-block behind my property and built on it. Registering at the local employment office I began looking for work, without success. Deciding I needed to be pro-active I contacted a drug and alcohol detoxification and rehabilitation centre run by a non-profit organisation and asked if I could do voluntary work there. The manager arranged for me to come in to discuss it and days later I was helping the detox supervisors.

Within a few weeks of starting at the centre the manager offered me a paid position as a relief detox supervisor - to fill in when others were on annual leave or sick. The job included shift-work so was physically as well as emotionally challenging, but I loved working there and learnt a lot. It also confirmed what I had begun to notice earlier, that I enjoyed jobs which were people-oriented rather than clerical work.

The detox and rehab centre consisted of a number of old buildings on a large block. One housed the administration offices while the main sprawling building was divided into two separate areas. The detox unit was a hospital-ward type room where people were admitted for sobering up. They remained there for a day or two and were looked after by the detox supervisors, who would regularly check on them and supply them with water and meals. A cook prepared meals for all the residents and staff in the centre. After this sobering-up period the client could either be discharged or, if interested in undergoing residential rehabilitation, be referred to a counsellor for assessment. Those accepted for the rehabilitation program would remain at the centre for a week or two, attending alcohol education classes and counselling. They would then be transferred to a rehab farm on the outskirts of Perth for three months. For many the detox unit was simply a safe place to sleep off a bender, but for others it was the beginning of their long road back to sobriety.

Almost all of the detox supervisors were graduates of a rehab program. As people began to sober up they would sometimes feel a need to talk to someone about their lives and problems. When they discovered that we'd also had problems dealing with alcohol in the past they became more relaxed about talking to us, knowing we understood something of what they were going through.

At times there was the belligerent drunk to deal with, but I never personally experienced any actual violence. However, we were all aware of the potential dangers. Quite often the police would deliver people to us to sober up instead of locking them up for the night, but only those who weren't aggressive.

My experience as a detox supervisor would be a factor in helping me to get another, longer-term job many years later. However, a more important and life-changing event was to happen because of my time there. Shortly after becoming a paid member of the team I met Glen, another casual staff member who would fairly soon become the father of my child.

Chapter Eleven

Approximately a year after meeting Glen we were living together and I was learning that the term "morning sickness" was grossly misleading, as it actually lasted all day. I was too sick to even leave the house for a few weeks, so it was fortunate that I had already resigned from my job. By the beginning of the second trimester I was feeling much better. I enjoyed watching my stomach getting steadily bigger and delighted in the experience of being pregnant and growing a tiny human being.

Sometime during the second trimester, probably soon after the morning sickness had disappeared, I had a sudden insight. I realised it was the first time in my life that I was actually happy being a woman, because I was able to experience the wondrous miracle of being pregnant. And although I often wore maternity dungarees as my stomach became too big for my normal clothing choice of jeans, I also felt more relaxed wearing dresses than I had pre-pregnancy. My feminine side had taken over and I was completely okay with that. I didn't let it get too carried away though - any time I wore lipstick I still considered myself in full make-up. My mascaras, powders and eye-shadows, etc. had been relegated to the bin years earlier and weren't about to be replaced.

Although I was very excited about impending

parenthood, as was Glen, the cracks in our relationship were already beginning to show. We were now living in my house and the tensions and arguments seemed to be increasing. By the time I was approximately seven months pregnant I decided the situation was impossible. Feeling that my ever-rising stress levels were bound to be having a negative effect on our unborn child, I moved into a tiny self-contained apartment that was attached to Mum and Dad's house. Luckily it was between tenants and available. I told Glen he could stay in my house until he found somewhere else to live, and then I would be selling it. The house was now filled with bad memories for me and I couldn't imagine wanting to live there again. As it was very old and only partially renovated, it wasn't capable of getting decent rent if kept as an investment.

Glen was very unhappy about this, and was determined for us to get back together. He moved out of my house after finding a suitable place to rent. We stayed in contact during the rest of my pregnancy, and he drove me into the hospital when I went into labour.

After a very difficult labour, which ended in an emergency caesarian section, Shaun was born two weeks early. He was tiny, as I had apparently developed undiagnosed pre-eclampsia during the last stages of the pregnancy. But apart from his low birth weight, luckily he was healthy.

Seeing Shaun for the first time, with his black hair and one tiny fist clenched against a flawlessly smooth cheek, I felt an incredible wave of love and protectiveness towards him. The overwhelming intensity of my emotions stunned me. I suddenly understood completely why most parents would die to protect their children if the situation demanded it.

The relationship between Glen and I improved after Shaun's birth. I felt I owed it to Shaun to see if there was any chance of reconciliation with his father, so we spent the weekends at Glen's place. He would drive over to collect us from our apartment at Mum and Dad's place on Friday nights and return us on Sunday afternoons. This arrangement continued for two or three months until, after continual pressure from Glen to do so, we moved back in with him. He was renting a modern three-bedroom duplex in a suburb almost an hour's drive from the apartment, a distance from family which would soon feel much further. Although I had some doubts about the wisdom of returning, I felt it was important for Shaun to have his father in his life. Despite everything that had gone before, there was still a strong emotional connection between Glen and I.

Unfortunately, although perhaps predictably, almost as soon as Shaun's and my belongings were unpacked, the problems and issues which had plagued the relationship the first time around returned.

Before Shaun was born I had sold my house. Prior to moving back to Glen's I had put an offer on another property, an old but well maintained two bedroom plus sleep-out asbestos house on a large flat block. My intention now I was again living with Glen was to rent it out. I only had a very small mortgage which would be covered by the rental payments, but these plans changed before finding tenants. Within months of returning, the living situation with Glen had become unendurable and my already fragile emotional state was deteriorating by the day. I felt that the constant tension and conflict would also be damaging for Shaun, as babies are very sensitive to the emotions of those around them. I knew we had to get away. When Shaun was approximately five months old we moved out and into my house.

Glen and I would end up having an off and on again relationship for the next seven or so years, but we would never live together again.

After Shaun was born my feelings about my gender became a little more complicated. I was still uncomfortable with my female body and felt that life would have made more sense if I had been a man. However, now I had my beautiful son I no longer regretted having been born a woman because if I had been a man Shaun would never have existed. Being a "Kate" instead of a "Karl" was a small price to pay for having Shaun. I was sure my maternal instincts were just as strong as any woman's and I would not swap being Shaun's mother for anything. However, now that Shaun had been safely born into the world, if the Gender Fairy had come along at that point and completely transitioned me into a physical man from that moment on, I would have been overjoyed.

Chapter Twelve

The emergency caesarean section I had undergone when Shaun was born had gone drastically wrong, with the epidural anaesthetic failing to work properly. The surgeon had initially refused to believe my anguished protests that I could feel the scalpel slicing through my abdomen and had continued cutting. After minutes that passed like hours, he belatedly acknowledged that I was actually experiencing pain and paused the operation so that a general anaesthetic could be administered before he continued.

So to paraphrase the words of Charles Dickens, our best of times can also simultaneously be our worst of times. Becoming a mother and taking the first tentative steps in the journey of getting to know and nurture my tiny, wonderful son was the most incredible experience of my life. At the same time however, I was in emotional shock, the results of the events during the caesarean. For the entire week that Shaun and I spent in the hospital maternity ward I felt very disoriented. It was as if reality had suddenly shifted in some indefinable way, but only for me, no-one else seemed to have noticed. Perhaps the closest I can come to describing the mental and emotional confusion I felt was being the equivalent of an actor suddenly finding the script had been changed mid-movie. Her lines had been removed from it, so she was expected to make it up as she went along. Meanwhile, the rest of the cast was working from the original version and assumed she was too - not realising she was struggling to cope.

Although I had told my family what had happened during the operation I could not adequately explain how upset and confused I was by it. They were horrified when they heard of my ordeal, but naturally did not realise the full extent of the emotional after-shocks it was having on me. I didn't know how to explain to them the overwhelming sensation of feeling battered and broken, both physically and emotionally.

Despite being seen by a doctor as part of normal post-operative care, nothing was mentioned about what had happened in the operating theatre. It was as if it had never occurred, and I was too traumatised to raise the issue with either the doctor or nurses. Dad spoke to my doctor and asked why the epidural hadn't worked properly. Apparently the needle had been inserted too far up my back by the anaesthetist, thus markedly reducing its effectiveness. I cringe to think of the pain level if it hadn't worked at all.

During the week in hospital I assumed the nurses were aware of what had happened during my operation, but of course they probably had no idea. I imagine that everyone in the operating theatre that day would have avoided telling anyone else about the incident to avoid possible legal or other repercussions later on.

Although the experience of feeling a scalpel slice deeply across and into my abdomen was traumatic, if events from that moment on had unfolded differently

. I'm quite confident that I would have recovered from the distress of it fairly quickly. However, when the surgeon ignored my protests and had continued cutting, telling me that of course I wouldn't be feeling it, he had sent me the message that I was of no importance whatsoever. It was as if my pain and wishes were meaningless and I had once again become invisible, my voice unheeded. The later lack of acknowledgement that anything unusual had happened and the complete disinterest in whether or not I was coping, increased the emotional damage and my sense of worthlessness.

The fact that my suffering had been caused by professionals who were supposed to help people, not harm them, also added to the level of emotional trauma I was experiencing. Most of my family felt I would be justified to seek legal advice, but I knew I didn't have the emotional resources to cope with any further stress.

Unfortunately my emotional state didn't improve when Shaun and I went home. I developed clinical depression and post-traumatic stress disorder. (The post-traumatic stress disorder was initially diagnosed as post-natal depression and wouldn't be recognised for what it was until years later.) I was in a constant state of acute anxiety, and it was a daunting challenge to even venture out in public. Whenever surrounded by strangers in a busy shopping centre or simply walking along a quiet street I felt very vulnerable to physical assault, either upon Shaun or myself. The logical part of me knew the chances of this happening were extremely remote, but this didn't rid me of the fear.

My exaggerated fears for Shaun's safety stopped me from being able to take him to major shopping centres unless accompanied by another adult. I wasn't confident in my ability to keep him safe from the innumerable dangers I was certain lay in wait in a crowded public space. Glen was scornful of my anxieties but fortunately my parents and Sarah were more understanding. They knew my fears were excessive, but also realised I could not overcome them at that stage so generously accompanied Shaun and me whenever we needed to venture into "the danger zone". Shaun was four years old before I finally found the courage to take him to the cinema, which was situated in the nearby shopping complex, without a back-up team. The movie was "Toy Story" and the first one Shaun saw on the big screen, so it was a big milestone day for both of us. Afterwards we had lunch in the foodhall before browsing in the toy departments of various shops. By the time we returned home I was mentally exhausted but also elated that a psychological barrier had finally been overcome. The excursion had been stressful but less so than I had expected. At times I had actually enjoyed it, especially seeing Shaun's delight while watching the movie. He also seemed very pleased to have me to himself in an environment outside our home and I felt guilty that I hadn't been able to give him this type of experience much sooner.

The depression which had descended days after Shaun's birth became more severe over time and refused to be shifted by medication or counselling. Admittedly the counselling was very short-lived, as I was very unhappy about the counsellor I had chosen to see. The experience so disillusioned me with the whole therapy concept that it put me off trying again with anyone else.

I'm not sure now how long after the operation it was when it first happened, but at some point, even sleep no longer provided relief from my negative emotions. I began having extremely vivid nightmares which felt as clear as if I was awake. Although the minor details were usually different each time, most nights I would be plunged into a threatening scenario where I was physically attacked or was at risk of being so. One recurring nightmare had me trying to find my way through a maze of dark, seedy streets full of dangerous looking men. This would then develop into being chased and shot at by one or more people with guns. Other nights I would wake up terrified and gasping for breath after being kicked, punched or stabbed in the stomach in my alternate dream-world. Presumably, these nightmares were symbolic of my hospital experience and subsequent fears. These intensely realistic experiences occurred on an almost nightly basis for many months. Fortunately, they gradually became less frequent over time, but for years afterwards I would sometimes be violently ambushed during my nocturnal slumbers.

Mum and Sarah both provided me with a great deal of much-needed practical and emotional support in the years after Shaun's birth. This was despite Sarah also dealing with her own serious health issues for much of the time. I deeply appreciated them being there for me in my time of need, as without their help I really don't think I would have coped at all.

As the years went by, with most days simply a struggle to get through, I despaired of ever being able to break through the mental cage my emotions had imprisoned me in. Years earlier, at the age of eighteen, I had fully realised for the first time how limited my life was, due to various psychological problems, and had taken action to try and resolve them. The next eleven years had been a journey of personal growth, often painful and at times heading in the wrong direction, but overall, successful in that I had learnt how to engage with life.

Now the gains made during those years had all been lost and I wasn't at all confident that I would be able to recover them. The journey of my youth could not be duplicated and nor would I have wanted to tread that path again. But what I could do again was take emotional risks. I knew that if there was to be any chance of getting my life back on track I had to step outside my shrunken so-called comfort zone and face my fears, just as I had as a teenager.

Chapter Thirteen

Desperate to break out of my emotional chains, I spent considerable time and effort trying to work out how to go about it, before finally deciding to apply to study at university. Hopefully, if successful this would have two major benefits, providing a way of re-entering the wider world in a structured, safe environment as well as gaining qualifications for getting a job later on.

I was very interested in the criminal justice system, so applied to Edith Cowan University for entry into the Bachelor of Arts, Justice Studies course. I was accepted and began in February, four years after Shaun was born. For the first semester I only enrolled in a single unit and Mum minded Shaun at my house on the one day a week I attended class. Having completed the Diploma of Teaching years earlier, I was able to get exemptions for half the course, saving considerably on time and tuition fees. Getting to the campus involved taking a bus and train as I was still not driving at this stage, due to my on-going anxiety issues.

My nervousness in the early days of teacher's college so long ago was nothing compared to the anxiety levels in the first weeks of university. But coupled with this fear was the excitement of knowing I was beginning to stretch the constricted boundaries of my life. It was also good to once again be in the academic environment, learning about new subjects and being intellectually challenged.

Although the majority were straight out of high school there were enough mature-age students to enable me to blend in. A number of the older ones were attending part-time, already employed in various branches of the justice system as police, prison, and community corrections officers. They would often share with the class interesting anecdotes about their experiences. It took me five years to complete my degree. For some of that time I didn't attend at all, due to shifting house and later having a stress fracture in my back, but for a couple of semesters I went almost full-time.

During those years I overcame the worst of my fears, once again able to leave the house without panicking, and I resumed driving, but I had by no means regained my previous confidence level. I'm not sure exactly when, but at some stage in the early months of going into public on my own more regularly, I began to experience episodes of "dissociation". These attacks would usually come on very suddenly, when I would experience a strange and unnerving alteration in my consciousness. A disembodied feeling would engulf me, making it feel as if body and mind were operating separately. This would be accompanied by a very faint noise filling my head, similar to the static of a badly tuned radio. My field of sight would also constrict, reducing to tunnel vision. At the same time an invisible mental wall would form between me and my surroundings, causing a dream-like sensation. Many of my actual dreams felt more real than it did during the more intense episodes. I would also be unnerved by the frightening and contradictory belief that I was virtually invisible to those around me, while at the same time being convinced those same people were staring at me.

During severe attacks it was very difficult to interact with other people, the dream-like quality of the situation making it hard to function naturally and automatically. The fear that my inner confusion was perhaps showing itself outwardly, making my behaviour seem odd, would increase the severity of the attack. The only way to short-circuit them was to leave the situation as quickly as possible, preferably going home if I could.

These episodes never occurred at home or while visiting family or friends. Although most of them happened while in shopping centres, occasionally they would occur while on the train or even when walking between classes at university. I seemed to be more likely to have an episode if I was particularly nervous about a situation or not feeling well. In order to cope with the emotional overload I think my brain would partly disengage itself, hoping to reduce the stressful stimuli.

During my studies I had to give three oral presentations to my tutorial groups as part of my assessments. Not surprisingly, the attacks would hit each time as my anxiety levels sky-rocketed.

Ironically, this disembodied dream-like sensation which made it feel as if someone else was speaking was probably what carried me through the ordeals. In those instances my brain's partial shut-down strategy actually helped rather than hindered.

I enjoyed the academic side of university, with the exception of oral presentations, but I wasn't able to overcome my shyness and insecurity. I did get to know some of the other mature-age students well enough to occasionally join them in the cafeteria for lunch or coffee breaks, but most of my time out of class was spent doing research in the library. The depression which had become a part of every-day life stubbornly refused to go away, but it did noticeably improve once I began university.

Early on in my studies I'd had serious concerns about my emotional ability to work in this field. There were times when my doubts were so strong that I began to research other options in entirely different fields. But nothing captured my enthusiasm and I felt strongly that for some reason the criminal justice area was where I was meant to be. Because of this deep gut instinct it was then fairly easy to believe that the courage would be there when I needed it. It was Sarah who pointed this out, that I had to let go and the future would take care of itself if, as seemed to be the case, I was meant to be studying in this field.

I sat my final exam in November 1999 and was then ready and eager for the next step - to begin looking for a job within the criminal justice area. After a year of unsuccessfully looking for work, I was delighted when I received a phone call from the senior community corrections officer at one of the community justice centres. He asked if I could come in for an interview the following Monday as there was a short-term position as a community corrections officer available. The next chapter of my life was about to begin.

Chapter Fourteen

My interview for the eight week community corrections officer (CCO) position was successful and I began work on the Friday. It had been more than ten years since I had been in paid employment so I was a tad nervous to say the least.

The manager showed me around the centre, introducing me to my new workmates as we went, with everyone offering a friendly welcome. The office was divided into cubicles by grey chest-high partitions, each occupied by two CCO's. Offenders were interviewed in small two-door rooms containing a desk, chairs and a hidden panic button. If pressed, the button would immediately activate an alarm in the general office area as well as the local police station. This piece of information was either disturbing, or re-assuring, depending on how you looked at it.

The first day was spent with the woman whose job I would be doing for two months. I sat in with her while she interviewed offenders - or clients, as we were to refer to them - and she summarised the duties of the position. One of the main functions of the CCO was to supervise offenders who had either been released from prison and were currently on parole, or had been given a community supervision order by the courts.

The CCO ensured that the offender reported to the office regularly and that they were complying with any other requirements of their order, such as substance or psychological counselling. The other major aspect of the job was writing pre-sentence and parole reports for the courts and parole board. The CCO interviewed the offender, either in prison or in the office, gathering background information from them and other sources before providing the report to the relevant authority.

      Much of the first week was spent interviewing clients as they reported, writing reminder letters to those who failed to show up when due, and reading through their files. Each person on an order had their own file which included court histories, reports written on them, copies of correspondence and details of their current obligations. Some people had two or three volumes to their files, showing records of lives which were dominated by criminal behaviour dating back decades to their youth and years spent in prison. Most of the offenders in the system had very dysfunctional childhoods, with many having endured physical, emotional and/or sexual abuse. A significant proportion of the women had been sexually abused as children, often by step-fathers or male relatives. Their files were depressing to read and made me realise just how lucky I and most other people had been to grow up in a loving, supportive family. If I hadn't been able to return to the safe haven of my home and family during my dark times as a teenager in Queensland, I dread to think where my life could have headed.

Although the workload was high and the issues we dealt with were often emotionally draining, I enjoyed the job very much. It was also a relief to find that I could cope with the various challenges that came with it.

Interviewing clients was nerve-wracking at first, but as I became more used to it I began to relax. I also liked writing reports for the courts and parole board, enjoying the process of gathering information from the offender and other sources. Often, convicted offenders would be remanded in custody while waiting to be sentenced, which meant the CCO assigned to write their report for the judge would have to interview them in prison. It was a strange experience entering an area surrounded by towering, razor-wire topped stone walls and knowing that getting out again was totally dependent on other people opening doors and gates. It must be very claustrophobic for the prisoners, seeing other people coming and going while they are cut off from the world.

At the community justice centre offenders could sometimes be heard shouting at their officers in the interview rooms, putting us all on alert, but there were no actual incidents of violence while I worked there. A few years later, when I was working at another office, I thought I was about to be physically attacked when an offender I was interviewing suddenly stood up, began yelling obscenities and leaned over me, his fists clenched. Luckily another staff member heard what was happening, quickly came into the room and helped me talk the offender down before he threw a punch. I felt very shaken up after such a near miss, and shocked at how quickly the situation had escalated to that point.

Although I still found it difficult to interact easily with the mothers at school or in new social situations, somehow once at work everything became simpler. I even found it quite easy, after the first week or so, to chat and joke with my workmates and form friendships. Perhaps it was because the role of CCO was defined - I knew what was expected and simply followed the script.

I had decided, when beginning my job with the department, that I would always wear trousers or jeans to work. I still always felt much more comfortable in these than in a dress or skirt and luckily, because of the sort of job it was, long pants were considered totally appropriate. Some of the other women also always wore pants while others mixed it up a bit. I had very rarely donned a dress or skirt since I'd had Shaun, and only then when I felt the occasion positively insisted on something formal. The last time I wore a dress to one of these occasions I was very conscious of the extra weight I was carrying around my middle. My self-consciousness turned to outright alarm when I saw myself in the mirror and realised I was so wide in the beam that I looked like a tugboat. All that was missing was a foghorn. I promised myself then that once the event was over and I was safely back in my own harbour, I would never wear a dress or skirt again, no matter what the fashion police did to me.

I didn't like wearing them, and now that I realised they weren't doing my appearance any favours either, they had to go.

Even though my clothing choice was nothing unusual in the office, the fact that I considered that I was in full make-up if I was wearing lipstick probably was. Never wearing shoes or sandals with any heel to speak of was also probably unusual. Although none of my fellow female workmates ever commented, they must have noticed. When any of them were handing party-plan beauty product catalogues around the office I was rarely offered a peek at any of them, not out of any attempt to exclude me, but simply because they correctly assumed that I wouldn't be interested. Even in my late teens when I was learning how to wield a mascara brush without taking out an eye, I wasn't overly interested in make-up for its own sake. I was really only interested in the end result. The only part I did actually enjoy was applying nail polish.

At the end of the initial eight week acting period my employment contract was extended for another month, because the woman I was replacing was not ready to return. Most of the CCO's in the office were also on short-term contracts, which didn't provide any sense of job security. Four months after beginning the job I was still there on yet another extension and at this point I belatedly attended the mandatory four day formal CCO training course. Fortunately, a few years later this policy was improved considerably, so that new recruits received three months formal training on all aspects of the job before actually being let loose in the office to sink, swim, or thrash about as best they could.

Just over a year after beginning work with the department I was made a permanent employee. I was assigned to a number of different centres as a relief officer before being given my permanent inner city posting when a vacancy came up. One of the centres I was temporarily assigned to was situated virtually next door to the local magistrate's court and the duty community corrections officer was expected to attend there if needed. Sometimes the magistrate would request a verbal rather than a written pre-sentence report, as well as the occasional breach report if an offender had not been complying with his or her order.

I desperately hoped nothing of the sort would come up while I was the duty officer, but a couple of weeks after starting at the centre I was given the news I dreaded. I was to interview an offender who had just reported to the centre, and the next day present a verbal pre-sentence report about him to the magistrate. Because he knew I hadn't done this before, one of the senior community corrections officers, Fred, said he would come and sit in the court with me.

Somehow I managed to stand up in court the following day and present my report, but only barely. While I had been waiting for the magistrate to call on me, sitting there in a puddle of anxiety, I was suddenly attacked by the all too familiar removed from reality feeling. Luckily the offender and I were called on moments later, before the attack had time to escalate too far. I could hear the tremor in my voice as I spoke and knew that fear was reducing my delivery to a strangled monotone. But as it was all I could do to get the words out, I was beyond caring how they sounded. The ordeal left me quite shaken for the rest of the day, but by the following morning I was okay again.

The next week, as I once again began my turn as duty officer, Fred casually advised me that I would need to go over to the courthouse in an hour or so and present a breach report. The offender was on bail and would be at the court, so I could interview him before his case was called up. Breach reports were even more daunting than pre-sentence ones, as they often involved a large amount of information, including various dates which had to be totally accurate.

I was soon at the courthouse and in a small interview room with the offender I was to give the report on. I had been in a steadily increasing state of anxiety ever since being given my assignment, and as I wrote down the young man's answers to my questions I felt the beginning of a dissociation attack coming on. It became difficult to concentrate on what I was being told and I hoped I was recording the information accurately. Once the interview was finished I asked him to return to the waiting area. As soon as he left I sat there desperately trying to get my perceptions back to normal. It was no use, my head was filled with static, I couldn't see properly and all effective thought processes had just about completely shut off. I knew I wouldn't be capable of going into the courtroom and presenting the report, so rang my senior, Fred. I told him I needed his help, and he said he would come straight over, arriving minutes later. My distress must have been obvious because Fred didn't argue when I told him I wasn't well and couldn't stand up in court. Without comment he re-interviewed the offender – who must have been wondering what was going on – and then told me I could sit in the public gallery and watch the proceedings.

I was still unnerved by the day's events as I drove home that evening, but told myself I would be okay again tomorrow. However, the following morning I was still shaken up and rang in sick, not feeling focused enough to be able to deal with the demands of the job. It was as if I had been catapulted back into the emotional state of years previously, when the world felt like a very threatening and frightening place. All of my self-confidence had disappeared, I couldn't complete a line of thought, and the prospect of returning to work and having to interview offenders was nerve-wracking.

I had previously assumed that I had recovered from my post-traumatic stress disorder because my dissociative episodes had disappeared, I was confident enough to interview offenders, do prison visits and generally function in society. I now realised that it had just been lying dormant, ready to emerge again if given the right circumstances. My first court appearance a week earlier had been the initial trigger, as the combination of public speaking and having to do so in a formal legal setting had filled me with fear. The fact that I had been unable to remove myself from the situation had made it much worse. I would have had to draw attention to myself by pushing past Fred and others seated in the row. Being in a frightening situation combined with no reasonable avenue of escape from it was too similar to my hospital experience. Probably if I hadn't been told a week later that I would have to stand up in court again it would soon have simply been an unpleasant memory, but the prospect of having to repeat the experience was apparently too much to shrug off.

I made a doctor's appointment and after I explained how I was feeling she gave me a medical certificate to cover three weeks sick leave. I didn't have any further dissociative episodes during my time off work and was relieved that the depression, which was always present to some degree, didn't deepen. By the time my three weeks sick leave was up, I was due to begin my next relief position at another centre, which thankfully was not connected to a magistrate's court. Shortly after that, in December 2002, I was given my permanent spot in an inner-city office, again without any court attached.

Chapter Fifteen

    I soon got to know my new colleagues and became familiar with the routines of the office, but still didn't feel back to my usual self. The undercurrent of anxiety which had returned after the court incident was still there and the confidence built up over the past two years of employment remained severely eroded. Although I had always found the strict deadlines for the written court and parole reports somewhat stressful, they were now much more so. I no longer had confidence in my ability to get reports done on time, despite the fact that I had never been late with one. It was also difficult to concentrate and to write with as much detail and analysis as I had previously. Although still of an acceptable standard I knew they weren't indicative of what I had previously been capable of, which further reduced my morale. Seeing the clients when they reported for supervision became another source of anxiety as I had also lost confidence in being able to help them work out strategies to deal with their various issues. I began to feel like a fraud, trying to help others when I didn't even know how to deal with my own problems.

    The dissociative episodes were ambushing me at random intervals and in varying intensities. A few times I had mild attacks while interviewing people, and I had to end the sessions as quickly as possible.

Probably because of these various issues my depression, which had for a fairly long period just been a low background hum, gradually intensified.

I eventually decided I needed professional help and reluctantly attempted counselling again. I wasn't very hopeful after my previous experience years earlier, but knew I needed to at least give it another chance. After a couple of false starts I found a psychologist, Dr B, I was happy with. Dr B restored my confidence in the psychological counselling profession. Over the course of approximately eighteen months he helped to reduce the chronic anxiety I felt about the operation. Unfortunately, our sessions couldn't seem to break the stranglehold of general anxiety and depression which once again dominated my life.

As well as seeing Dr B, I began taking anti-depressant medication. It hadn't worked in the past but I was desperate enough to try again. After trying a number of different types in an attempt to find one without side-effects and that actually worked, I discovered one which eased the depression slightly. Even these stopped working completely after a short while so I abandoned the medication route once and for all.

Over the course of two years I alternated with struggling to cope at work, and, when it all became too overwhelming, taking periods of sick leave. (Mostly unpaid leave, as I had quickly used up my annual entitlements.) I even voluntarily moved to a lower level position on a temporary basis, which still required dealing with offenders, but had less responsibilities overall.

Importantly, I didn't have to write court and parole reports. For me these had become one of the most difficult aspects of the community corrections officer role, partly due to the uncompromising deadlines involved. Despite the easier duties of my new job, my emotional state made it a daily struggle to cope.

Sometimes, while at my desk struggling to focus on paperwork, I found myself wondering if everything would be less stressful if I was a man. I would let my imagination take over, picturing myself sitting there at my desk as a man, and mentally interacting with my colleagues from this male position. This imaginary gender change was rather painful, as blatantly unattainable fantasies often are. But as my emotional state became more fragile, I often found myself thinking along these irrational lines, that being a man would somehow magically allow me to overcome my anxieties, and to cope with life.

In April 2004 I had begun one of my many periods of sick leave, as I was experiencing a particularly severe bout of depression and anxiety which made going to work impossible. It was around this time that Sarah lent me a copy of a spiritual book she had just read, titled "The Power of Now" by Eckhart Tolle. She strongly encouraged me to read it, explaining that it had a lot of information on how to let go of past negative experiences and live life in the present moment. She assured me that this book stood out amongst all the others and had made a huge impact on her thinking. Despite Sarah's high recommendation I wasn't very hopeful that it would be able to help much, if at all.

I had read quite a few self-help and spiritual books in the past, and although some of them were inspirational and helpful in making small improvements to my life, these changes were short-lived. There were no transformational breakthroughs - I could never seem to change my basic low self-image or coping skills. Despite this, I recognised that many of the books in these genres were very worthy and had helped countless other people improve their lives. However, I found they often left me feeling more inadequate because I couldn't turn my life around using the ideas and strategies they recommended.

So after my initial reluctance to try yet another spiritual book, I began to read "The Power of Now" and within a couple of chapters found it hard to put down. I found certain parts of it quite confronting, in that it made me look at how my own distorted thinking was creating the severe emotional pain I was suffering. Without realising it, I had made the operation and the resulting post-traumatic stress disorder and depression into a large part of my identity. Many of my current emotions were still a reaction to what had happened on the operating table, as if that event defined who I was from then on. Reading about Eckhart Tolle's ideas, I could see the truth of what he was saying, but still felt that my emotional problems were too big to ever rid myself of them totally.

Sarah bought me my own copy of the book so that I could keep re-reading it, assuring me that each time I would get something new out of it. For a while there was no real shift in my emotional state, but at some point during the next few months I had a partial breakthrough. My attitude about the operation changed. Although my sessions with Dr B had helped a lot in dealing with the painful memories, I still couldn't talk about the events of that day without becoming upset. After reading Tolle's book a few times I suddenly "got it" emotionally as well as intellectually, and the operation was no longer important. I could leave it in the past where it belonged. It did not define who I was and the only place it still existed was inside my head. When I fully embraced this and let go of the operation I could, for the first time, talk about it without getting upset.

A more important benefit was that my dissociation attacks totally disappeared, making it much easier to go out alone in public. I felt these were big steps forward, but my severe depression and general anxiety remained and I feared that nothing would be capable of ridding me of them. In fact, they appeared to be getting worse. Many times I would wake up in the early hours of the morning sick with anxiety and hopelessness, wondering how I was ever going to find my way back to mental health.

Shaun was now in his first year of high school and finding the transition from primary school difficult, especially since most of his friends from the previous years were now in different schools. I was worried that he was often getting depressed, and decided we could both do with a short holiday as a circuit breaker. I hadn't forgotten that my previous attempts at fixing my problems by going away somewhere usually failed, but still hoped that this time it could work. Not surprisingly, Shaun thought it was a great idea.

I chose Brisbane as our destination, as it was a city I knew and therefore felt more confident about visiting. The few weeks between booking our trip and actually beginning the holiday were even more stressful than before, as I hoped I hadn't taken on more than I could cope with. I had never been so far away from family support if needed while at the same time being solely responsible for Shaun's welfare. During my really bad moments I feared I would have a total nervous breakdown in Brisbane. I kept telling myself I should be able to hold it together for the short time we would be away - even if I fell apart the moment we got back.

On the 3rd November 2004 Mum and Dad drove Shaun and me to the airport and as we walked through the terminal, excitement and anticipation began to override the anxiety. Stepping onto the plane a short time later, I had no way of knowing just how life-changing this trip was to be.

Chapter Sixteen

It is often said that the darkest hours are just before the dawn, and for me, in an emotional sense, this was very true. In the weeks before Shaun and I flew to Brisbane I had fallen into such a deep pit of depression that I seriously doubted whether it would be possible to ever be happy again. Somehow I would just have to endure the rest of my life as best I could, but it stretched as a bleak and joyless road - and then something completely unexpected and wonderful happened for me in Brisbane.

The day after we arrived, as Shaun and I were sitting in a cafe having lunch and idly chatting, I suddenly realised with a shock of surprise that my depression had totally disappeared. In its place was a strange sensation that after a few moments of mental probing I recognised as happiness, an almost forgotten emotion. The cripplingly severe anxiety that had previously pervaded everything was also missing. It had been replaced by a mild, very manageable version of itself.

The following week flew by, yet seemed to go on forever. Although half-expecting my depression and acute anxiety to return as suddenly as they had disappeared, they stayed away, and Shaun and I had a great time doing touristy things in and around Brisbane. To my surprise and delight, returning home didn't send my mood spiralling downwards again either, showing that my happiness wasn't simply due to being in Brisbane.

I had taken Eckhart Tolle's book with me to Brisbane as a security blanket. As it happened, I didn't even need to take it out of the case - it had already woven its magic. Having read various chapters of his book many times over the preceding months I must have absorbed more of Tolle's teachings than I had realised. My subconscious had been quietly learning the lessons without telling me what it was up to.

In Brisbane when I had realised my depression was gone I didn't immediately connect its disappearance with having read Tolle's book. It wasn't until weeks later that I began to suspect that The Power of Now was responsible. Now I have no doubt at all that it was due to reading this book in the preceding months that my depression disappeared. I can only guess as to why my mood changed virtually instantly once in Brisbane, rather than gradually over some time. Perhaps because I was in a new environment, my focus was more on my surroundings and less on how I was actually feeling. This gave my subconscious a chance to overpower the depression and acute anxiety using its newly learnt knowledge. If Shaun and I hadn't gone on this trip I'm assuming I would have still overcome the depression and anxiety, but it would probably have been a much slower process.

In the years since that miraculous time in Brisbane I have only had a few relatively short-term bouts of depression. I am still prone to anxiety, and sometimes have severe episodes of it. But these anxiety attacks can often be stopped or lessened by remembering Eckhart Tolle's principles.

Not surprisingly, after recovering from my depression and the extremes of anxiety I was able to function more effectively at work. However, I decided to remain in the lower-level position rather than return to being a community corrections officer (CCO). My current job was stressful, but the CCO role was much more so. Many CCO's were struggling to cope with increasingly high workloads, and some were finding other avenues of employment.

In January 2008 I had a minor heart attack. An angiogram showed that my arteries were clear so the cardiologist wasn't sure what had actually caused the attack. He thought it may have been an arterial spasm or a tiny blood clot. I was horrified by this, and for quite awhile afterwards felt very physically vulnerable.

I returned to work shortly after this, but was so exhausted by lunchtime each day that I could barely function. In addition, my ability to concentrate was almost non-existent, so after a few weeks I went to the doctor and was diagnosed with chronic fatigue syndrome. This condition can be triggered by a range of causes, including physical events, high stress levels, and viruses. So presumably the heart attack and the resultant stress of invasive diagnostic tests were the culprits in this case. Work had also been particularly stressful in the months leading up to my attack, so maybe this was another contributing factor.

. The doctor gave me a medical certificate and I went on unpaid leave yet again.

During 2008 my chronic fatigue ebbed and flowed in its severity, but it didn't improve enough to return to work. Some days I was confined to bed with exhaustion, while on others I felt almost well.

I finally returned to work in mid 2009. My illness hadn't gone but it was considerably improved. Because I still had very low energy levels I requested to change to part-time work of three days a week. This was approved but even these reduced hours were a challenge and I always went home at the end of the day mentally and physically drained. As well as having very little physical stamina the stresses of the job were very emotionally exhausting.

A few months after returning to work I became very ill with a virus. Extensive blood tests couldn't determine its identity, although the symptoms were similar to glandular fever. After a few weeks, when the virus had moved on, I was still very weak and exhausted but assumed I would slowly return to my usual state of health. This didn't happen, and when there was no improvement at all, I realised the virus had left me with a parting memento of its visit, having increased my mild chronic fatigue to a debilitating level.

Because I had been off work for so long over the previous years I was determined not to succumb to illness again and I returned to the office after a number of weeks. This proved to be a mistake and my health gradually deteriorated further as I pushed my body far beyond its current capabilities. My work suffered as I had virtually lost my short-term memory, I couldn't concentrate, and everything was done through a fog of extreme fatigue. Eventually I had to admit defeat. I knew I couldn't live with the responsibility of unwittingly causing problems for someone if I overlooked something vital or made a bad decision. Particularly as some mistakes could have legal consequences. I took unpaid sick leave, but after numerous extensions of that initial three months I resigned from my job, as my health stubbornly refused to show any improvement at all.

Chapter Seventeen

Although the exact time frame is hazy, it was somewhere in 2009 when I heard that Chaz Bono, the daughter of the singer Cher, was in the process of transitioning to male. This stunned me, as until that moment I'd had no idea that females could transition to males. I had seen the occasional reference on television to men who became women but I hadn't made the leap of logic to realise, or even wonder, if the opposite could occur. This sounds incredibly naïve, especially considering my own lifelong discomfort with my gender, and I am still surprised that such a possibility had stayed hidden under my radar until then. But perhaps it's not actually as surprising as it seems. Although now, in 2018, transgender issues and stories are often in the media, and this trend is growing in momentum all the time, it has only been in the past few years that this has been the case. I imagine that today most young people, by the time they leave their teens, would have learnt that people of both sexes can be transgender, and that some physically transition. In contrast, I, and presumably most of my peers, would not have come across any references to transgender people while we were growing up. Information was much harder to come by, and was more parochial than it is today.

Even with more attention paid to the transgender topic, the media still appears to focus predominantly on male-to-female transition than female-to-male. So, for those not paying close attention to the subject, perhaps it's still not blatantly obvious that women as well as men can be transgender, and that some of them also physically transition.

Being that Sarah was already privy to my gender issues, I told her about Chaz Bono's transition journey when I heard about it. As the conversation unfolded, the penny started to drop for both of us that maybe I too was transgender. Hard on the heels of that epiphany came another realisation. Because I like men, presumably that meant I was a gay transgender man. This actually made a lot of sense and I wondered how I could not have known until now. What a revelation.

For the next few days the over-riding and rather contradictory emotions were shock, disbelief, and relief. Relief, because so many puzzling and uncomfortable aspects of my life now made sense.

I had always believed that I wasn't very good at being a woman and had felt I was somehow inadequate because of this. I had always struggled with things that most other women seemed to find effortless, such as dressing in a feminine manner, or a multitude of other "female" skills that seemed to come naturally to others. I had also never really enjoyed girly chats about recipes or household management or the latest celebrity fashions and escapades. But, being that I was transgender, no wonder I didn't feel very adept at being a woman. Hopefully now that I recognised this, I would no longer feel stressed about my performance, and whether it was of an acceptable standard compared to other women.

During my late teens and early twenties I had tried to master the feminine arts of dressing attractively and navigating my way around a make-up kit. Even then however, I'd opt for jeans or shorts rather than skirts and dresses wherever possible, and only wore make-up in situations where it was almost a legal requirement. My favourite nightclubbing outfit was black skin-tight satin-look pants with a selection of dressy shirts, rather than a dress. I doubt that I have ever felt truly comfortable in a dress in my life, no matter how well it suited me. When I was eighteen I had one that I loved, a strapless cotton dress with a colourful tropical print. I wore it occasionally because I liked it so much, but I always felt vaguely uneasy in it.

All my life, getting dressed up for formal or special occasions had been stressful. As soon as I put on a formal dress and full make-up for a sophisticated night out I felt oversized and awkward, as if borrowing someone else's clothes. I am 5'7" and until my late twenties was very slim, so I was always puzzled by this discomforting feeling. For the entire evening I would feel like an imposter, someone trying to pass herself off as a fashionably dressed woman. I was convinced that people would be able to see right through the subterfuge. Until realising I was transgender I had no idea why I always got this unsettling feeling that I was a fraud whenever I got all dolled up for an occasion. Now of course, it makes sense.

This discomfort usually began during the shopping stage. I would optimistically choose a number of outfits from the racks in a women's clothing store and eagerly try them on in the change-rooms. However, as soon as I put one on and looked in the mirror, what had been an attractive, seemingly suitable choice suddenly appeared to be completely wrong, but I couldn't say why it was. Although not consciously aware of it, some part of me must have realised I felt like a man dressing up in women's clothing. It didn't feel right because what I really wanted was to be wearing a fancy suit rather than a fancy dress.

Although I wasn't comfortable with some aspects of the female job description, I did wholeheartedly enjoy many of the more traditionally feminine pursuits, such as sewing, and surrounding myself with attractive ornaments and objects. My childhood pursuits had not respected gender boundaries and this has continued throughout my life, as I still enjoy some of the more traditionally male interests as well as the female. I realise now how fortunate I am, that I was always able to connect with what there was of my feminine side. I know the pain of not being male-bodied would have been even more severe if I had only been interested in male pursuits to the exclusion of all else. Luckily for me my psyche is not, and never was, hyper masculine. Although I definitely feel male, I am considerably closer to the female side of the scale than many men would be. It is now becoming more apparent that gender is far more varied than simply being male or female. It has been said that perhaps there are as many different genders as there are people on the planet, as everyone experiences it differently. Some people even consider themselves to be genderless, not identifying with either male or female, while others feel they move between the genders.

As well as the sense of relief, it felt surreal that, the penny having finally dropped, I was now identifying myself as transgender. Until now it had been a label attached to a comparatively small number of other people, not myself. I had suddenly joined a group I had very little knowledge of. Even saying "I am transgender" to myself made me feel uncomfortable, as if trying on a new clothing style that I had never worn before. There was nothing wrong with the clothing, but it just didn't fit with the self-perception I had always had until then.

Throughout my life there had been very many clues as to my trans status. Some, like my desperate childhood longing to be a boy, were blatantly obvious, while others were more subtle. But because until now I'd had no idea that men could actually be trapped inside women's bodies, I was never able to put the pieces together to get the real picture. I had been given one of the more obvious clues years earlier, when watching a James Bond movie. A scene had come up showing Bond looking very dashing in a dinner suit and flirting with a beautiful and glamorous woman.

I had idly thought how nice it would be to be the type of woman to turn Bond's head. However, as soon as I had this thought I realised I wouldn't want to be a glamorous woman like that. Even if I could have been magically projected into the body of the woman dancing with Bond, I wouldn't want to be. I knew it wouldn't be a comfortable fit and I wouldn't know how to carry it off. I wouldn't even be interested in learning how to. I would rather be like Bond than the woman he was with. Of course, I didn't share his preference for women. Not only did I want to be like him - in most ways - but I wanted to be with men much like him.

      Another clue was to be found in one of my previous romantic relationships. Sometime during my years at teacher's college I had a brief relationship with Rohan who, although I didn't realise it at the time, was gay. From the beginning I felt more comfortable with him than I had ever felt with any of my previous romantic partners. Now, knowing my true identity, it is not surprising that the type of man I have felt most comfortable having a romantic relationship with would be gay. Unfortunately, although Rohan was the ideal partner for me both physically and emotionally, I came wrapped in the wrong physical package for him. We had only been going out together for a month or so when he realised it wasn't working for him and ended the relationship. I'm guessing I felt comfortable with him because presumably he wasn't trying to connect emotionally with the feminine in me, and at some deep level perhaps I sensed this. It was only later that I, and probably he, realised he was gay.

Although I have been physically attracted to males since the age of fourteen, sexual relationships have usually been emotionally uncomfortable for me. Being physically intimate with a partner means that the participants' bodies are the main focus for the duration of the exercise. In everyday situations I normally give as little thought as possible to my physical appearance, not wanting to be reminded of its femaleness. So when a partner is giving it his undivided attention because of its female form, I feel very self-conscious and uncomfortable. It's as if I've been sent onto the field in the wrong team's colours but, playing the game anyway, I'm cheered on as if I belonged in them. But because I don't want to be wearing those colours, the experience is very emotionally challenging. Because of this, I would have been quite happy having affectionate but non-sexual physical contact with my romantic partners, but unfortunately that's not usually how it works.

When I finally ended the relationship with Glen, Shaun's father, I was hoping it wouldn't be too long before I met another man. At that point I still had no idea that I was transgender, and assumed that my emotional discomfort when in romantic relationships was simply due to my lack of self-confidence. For a few years I went on the occasional date, but none of these went anywhere. It was soon after my depression lifted when I decided, at the age of 43, that I was actually happy not to have a partner. My relationships with men over the years had been, for the most part, difficult, and I decided that I was probably better off remaining single. It was a decision I've never regretted. Now, knowing who I am, I feel that a purely platonic but committed relationship with a man might work for me, but only if he saw me as a transgender man, and not a woman. As that is extremely unlikely, I assume I will be remaining (reasonably) content as a single.

Occasionally throughout my life I have dreamt that I was a man. In these nocturnal sleep scenarios I would sometimes realise that being male was a surprising turn of events, but a very welcome one. At other times I simply accepted my maleness as being normal and unremarkable as I got on with whatever adventures or misadventures my dream state conjured up for me. Always however, when I awoke and realised it was only a dream I felt a sharp stab of loss.

Long before my "aha moment," when idly leafing through advertising brochures which featured the latest clothing offerings, I would usually look at the men's selection after the women's. Sometimes I would choose a complete imaginary wardrobe from this section, imagining what I would buy to take on a holiday if I was a man. During these excursions into fantasy, I was always consciously thinking that it would be so much more fun, and easier, having a male body than a female, and buying men's clothes rather than women's. My determination as a teenager to repress my intense longing to be a male certainly hadn't been very successful. No matter what the situation, throughout my life I often instinctively saw it through the me-as-male perspective.

Now, attempting to come to terms with my newly discovered identity, I found myself going through a period of trying to find where I fit in the world, something that most of us do as teenagers. During my own adolescent struggle with this challenge I hadn't found the answer. My strategy at that time had been to forcibly try repressing my desperate longing to be male. Now, although I had more information, I was afraid I still wouldn't be able to find where I fit. In fact, this new knowledge, although very welcome, made everything seem even more confusing.

Realising how little I knew about transgender issues, I bought books written by trans people and avidly searched the internet for anything I could find on the subject. I discovered another world I had known virtually nothing about, and wondered how I had missed getting the memo about it for so long. It was a revelation to me that the first incidents of people physically transitioning from one gender to the other had occurred so long ago. One of the first documented cases of sex-reassignment surgery was that of Lili Elbe, a Danish painter. In 1930 she underwent the first of four risky surgical procedures to transform her body from male to female. Tragically, she died from complications following her fourth operation in 1931, just before her 49th birthday. She had been living openly as a woman for the last two decades of her life. Her story, which sadly didn't have the happy ending she deserved, was made into a book after her death.

    When looking for as much information about the transgender community as I could find, I was horrified at how much hate, violence and discrimination many trans people experience. I am in awe of the courage of Lili Elbe and the men and women who have come after her, daring to transition to their true selves, despite the often considerable risks to their physical and emotional safety.

    I felt liberated once I got my head around being transgender, and it made things easier in ways, but sometimes it also caused considerable pain. One day while returning to the office at the end of my lunch break, I saw two middle-aged men walking towards me, hand in hand. Looking at them I felt a sudden rush of emotion, a mix of happiness that these two men felt in a safe enough environment to openly declare that they were a couple, and an almost crippling grief that I would never, and could never, be in such a relationship. As we passed each other I was disconcerted to find myself actually trembling from the strength of my emotions.

    Over the next couple of years my transgender issues ebbed and flowed in their intensity, but were never far below my conscious attention. Sometimes I was emotionally ambushed when I least expected it. One evening I watched a television documentary about Freddie Mercury, the deceased gay lead singer of the rock group Queen. Queen had been one of my favourite bands when I was younger, and I loved Mercury's singing. I expected it to be sad, considering that Mercury had died young from AIDS, so I wasn't totally surprised when I found myself crying even before the point in the program when it began leading up to this. I was a little discombobulated however, when I realised I wasn't only crying for Mercury, but also for myself. While I was grieving that this wonderfully talented man was no more, I was also grieving that I could never physically be a gay man. No matter how much I felt like a man, I was still a woman as far as my body and the world was concerned. I admired immensely those transgendered men and women who had the courage to transition from one sex to the other, but I couldn't see myself ever doing the same - for many reasons. One of them being that I had been socialised as a female for approximately half a century and didn't think I could adjust to suddenly identifying socially as a male. I wouldn't know how to behave. Some people do successfully transition in their later years, but they must be far braver than I could ever be. If fantasy ever became reality and scientists were able to invent a magic pill that instantly physically transformed people into their correct gender, complete with appropriate social skills and knowledge, I would be the first in line. Failing that impossible turn of events I would remain physically female. I was hoping that once I got used to my new reality, the fact that I finally knew my true identity, even if the wider world didn't, would be enough. I suspected that this was simply wishful thinking, but hoped not. For now, I felt as if I was straddling two worlds but not really belonging to either.

Chapter Eighteen

Sometime during 2011, I decided to try writing a novel, casting one of my main characters as a transgender woman. I didn't get very far before abandoning it, worried that I wouldn't be able to give an accurate enough depiction of my transgender character. I also found that having to come up with a whole cast of well-thought-out characters and an attention-grabbing plot was beyond me, for now at least. I hoped that sometime in the future, once my health had improved, I might be able to try again. I also realised that I may just not be cut out to write a novel no matter how bouncing with good health I may be, but I wouldn't dwell on that possibility.

At the beginning of 2012 I was still semi-housebound due to my chronic fatigue, which was stubbornly refusing to go away or even loosen its grip on me. Desperate to feel that I was achieving something rather than just exist while I tried to get my health back, I became inspired to try writing again. This time however, it would be a narrative non-fiction book. I was worried that due to my continuing impaired short and medium-term memory I may not be able to write, but decided to try it and see. Although only able to work on it for very short stretches at a time, I found that writing my manuscript was a wonderful stress reliever. Writing became a very powerful form of relaxation therapy and I enjoyed virtually every minute. I managed to complete a very short manuscript in approximately sixteen months. Knowing that I was still capable of some sort of achievement despite my health restrictions boosted my confidence and spirits considerably.

Chapter Nineteen

In May 2014 Sarah asked me if I would like to come with her on a five-week holiday to the U.K. and Ireland. While there she would be visiting our brother Justin and his wife in Ireland, and attending a short health retreat in Somerset. My health was still very poor, although there had been mild but noticeable improvements in recent months. On my better days I was now able to do fifteen-minute walking sessions on my home treadmill, which was encouraging. Sarah and I thought that although the trip would be physically demanding, the emotional benefits of getting away to a new environment and having an exciting travel adventure might outweigh the negatives. Due to my very restricted social life and semi-housebound status because of my health, I was becoming mildly socially-phobic. Every time I did go out it was a bit of an emotional challenge and I didn't want this to be the start of the slippery slope back down into full-blown agoraphobia.

Sarah said she would be happy to go sightseeing on her own on the days I needed to stay resting in our accommodations, which we assumed would be fairly frequent. She also thought I might get a lot of benefit from attending the health retreat, to which I agreed. We were hoping the trip, which would require me to engage with the wider world again, would be good for my health, and I happily agreed to the idea.

It was a chilly mid-winter's night when we left Perth airport headed to Dublin, via Singapore and London. Neither of us could sleep on the plane and by the time we were halfway through our 13 hour flight from Singapore to London I was in considerable physical distress. Sarah was becoming alarmed at how ill I looked, and we were both silently wondering if my coming along was a huge mistake. To our surprise and relief I perked up considerably once we landed at London's Heathrow airport. While we were in the departure lounge waiting to board our plane to Dublin I had a brief hallucination. I thought a young man standing nearby was wearing a saddle and, rather than being surprised by his strange choice of attire, felt that it suited him. Within seconds I realised my mistake and saw that the saddle was actually a rucksack. So maybe I hadn't recovered as well as I had assumed. Sarah was also suffering the effects of the long flights by the time we landed in Dublin, but again to our surprise, after a good night's sleep we were both almost back to our respective normals.

After a week in Ireland, catching up with Justin and his wife before exploring Dublin, and a few days in Wales with friends of Sarah's, we arrived in London. Due to running on adrenaline-fuelled energy, I was able to do more sightseeing than I had hoped for, but I couldn't keep up with Sarah's pace, even though she had developed a severe case of bronchitis. So as expected, during our sixteen days in this magical city I needed to take a few days off from sightseeing and spent the time resting, relaxing, and reading in our hotel room while Sarah sallied forth on solo expeditions.

Chapter Twenty

After sixteen nights in London Sarah and I caught the train to Castle Carey and from there a taxi to Glastonbury, Somerset. This was where the health retreat we had pre-booked was due to begin the following day. Once we had checked into our accommodation we walked into the centre of town.

Although I had known Glastonbury was very alternative, I was still surprised by how strongly "not quite of this world" it felt. It didn't feel as if we were still in England, it had its own unique essence. Walking along what appeared to be the main street, we passed a trio of women dressed in exotic finery and discovered later that there was a goddess convention being held in the hall. The people on the street appeared to be an interesting mix of traditional lifestyle, and every-other-style, including a half-naked man with a longbow casually slung across his back. The Arthurian legends were set in this area and it still felt the type of place where a knight in shining armour riding down the street wouldn't be a total surprise to anyone. There was a wonderfully surreal atmosphere to the town and we loved it.

The retreat was both physically and emotionally energising. The other attendees came from a wide variety of backgrounds and countries, and the atmosphere was warm and inclusive.

    To my considerable surprise, on the third day I found myself revealing that I was transgender to Hugh, the facilitator of the retreat. In the few moments between telling him and getting his response to the information, my nerves were reduced to confetti. As I sat there, I wondered what on earth I had been thinking, to put myself in such an emotionally stressful and vulnerable situation. To my relief, Hugh's response was positive and we talked about it for a few minutes before he was called away to attend to some urgent matter.

    As we left the common room, Hugh told me if I wanted to talk more about it later I was welcome to. I thanked him and went to find Sarah. I was feeling almost euphoric, as I had actually shared my secret with someone else, and my listener had not been critical or disbelieving. Sarah had always been very accepting of my new found identity and very supportive, but this was the first time I had dared tell anyone else. Finding Sarah in our shared room, I told her about my conversation with Hugh. I explained how incredibly freeing and empowering it felt to have told him, and that he had been very encouraging. One of my fears of ever telling anyone else had been that my self-assessment about my actual identity would be discounted. Sarah had known for practically all her life that I had desperately wanted to be a boy when I was a child, and that I had always found it difficult trying to be like other women in many ways, so she knew my transgender issues were valid. But if I told anyone else, they would perhaps argue that I couldn't possibly be a man trapped inside a woman's body, and that I was weird to even suggest such a thing. Or alternatively, if they did accept that I really was transgender as I claimed, then maybe they would be horrified and disgusted. Hugh had immediately and unquestioningly accepted that I was actually a man in all but body, and this validation of my true identity was invaluable. And just as importantly, he also hadn't thought I was weird or some sort of freak.

The rest of the afternoon was free time so Sarah decided to do a sketch of the Abbey ruins which were in the centre of town. I decided to wander around the town again while she was sketching. I had no particular destination or plan in mind but I felt so energised I just needed to be moving. Walking along, my euphoria grew as I was feeling my male essence very strongly. And, perhaps for the first time, it wasn't being diluted by the contradictory awareness of my female body. I was entirely focussed on the mental, rather than on the body in which I was currently travelling. At last, I was fully embracing my transgender identity. Having someone who barely knew me accepting me as transgender without questioning its validity as an identity, allowed me to finally completely accept it myself.

As I was about to enter an interesting looking jewellery shop I passed two women who were so splendidly attired that I guessed they were attendees of the Goddess convention. What a wonderful concept, to have an event which celebrates the feminine when so much of society is slanted towards the masculine. Without warning, I felt a strange sense of loss. While delighting in fully embracing my maleness for the first time, I had just lost the last remaining emotional connection to my femaleness. Although obviously still physically female, my emotional self-identification had just fully completed the transition to the male. So now, looking at the two "goddesses" as they passed by, I no longer felt that I was a fellow woman. Although I had never felt comfortable or very proficient at being female and always knew I would rather have been a man, I had always been identified, by myself and others, as a woman. Now I had just been thrown out (or perhaps thrown myself out?) of a club which maintained strict criteria for membership and I no longer qualified. I was surprised at how much this affected me, although I knew that such a paradigm shift was bound to cause some emotional tremors. Luckily these negative emotions had no hope of overriding my euphoria, so they agreed to co-exist for awhile.

    Arriving back in London after the retreat was finished, Sarah and I caught a taxi from the station back to the hotel, not wanting to lug our large suitcases onto a busy tube train during rush hour. As the taxi made its way through the traffic I suddenly had the intense and disorienting sensation of just having come back to consciousness after a period of oblivion. It was as if I had just woken up from a very deep, dreamless sleep to find myself in a taxi. The past few days were vivid memories, but it didn't feel as if we had only left there this afternoon. In fact it felt as if our visit to Glastonbury and my experiences there could have been months ago. I was slightly unnerved as I tried to work out why I had this strong impression. Perhaps it was because the events of the past few days had been so different to any previous experiences I had ever had, and in Glastonbury, which was also unique and unlike anywhere I had been before. The event in Glastonbury, where for the first time I could totally accept and feel comfortable with being a transgender man, was a rebirth of sorts. So now having this strange sensation as if I was just waking up from a deep sleep felt symbolically very appropriate. Satisfied I probably wasn't going crazy after all, I turned my attention to watching the street scapes passing by.

Chapter Twenty-One

Sarah and I returned from our trip in early August, 2014. I still felt very connected to my inner maleness, emotionally identifying with it completely. Although I was very happy about this, it was not without pain. I was still seen as female by the rest of the world, and my female body meant that I remained straddled across two identities, not fully fitting into either. But I didn't have too much time to focus on my identity issues at that point.

Shortly before Sarah and I arrived back home our father had fallen over in our parents' backyard and broken his hip. He was still in hospital and we hoped he would be home soon. At the time of his fall Dad had been suffering from mild dementia and suspected Parkinson's. After the hip replacement operation Dad developed post-operative delirium. We learnt from extensive research on the Web afterwards, that it's a potential complication of general anaesthesia in those with dementia. This severely accelerated his dementia and he never regained his ability to walk more than a few halting paces again. After a couple of months he couldn't walk at all. On the advice of his doctors we admitted Dad into a nursing home in late October, when it was becoming clear his mental and physical state would only deteriorate from that point on. It was extremely distressing for all of us and it took a long time to emotionally adjust to what Dad's and our new reality was. Although Mum, Sarah and I had known, as had Dad, that his future looked grim and he may well eventually end up in a nursing home, suddenly that future was now and it was a horrible shock.

    Except for occasional, brief interludes of awareness, Dad had very little idea where he was or that he had dementia. He was like a child, distressed that he was in a situation he couldn't understand, and it was heart-breaking.

Chapter Twenty-Two

Ever since the turning point in Glastonbury I no longer felt the vague discomfort that I wasn't conforming to any socially imposed rules of being female which had stubbornly persisted until then. This new comfort with my maleness gave me the confidence to further modify my clothing choices. I had already stayed true to my determination never to wear a dress or skirt again, and hadn't been confined in one since late 2000. I had however, still often bought tops and jumpers that were quite girly. I was never totally at ease in these either, but until the Glastonbury episode, had persisted in my misguided attempts to look at least a little feminine at times, despite now knowing my true identity. Now I decided to clear out my wardrobe of virtually everything that more than hinted at being feminine. It was very liberating to finally work out what clothes made me emotionally comfortable and to only buy these. It also saved money as I was no longer buying tops that I had optimistically thought I would one day wear, only to leave them languishing in the far recesses of my wardrobe because I never felt comfortable in them.

The only make-up I had worn for decades had been lipstick, and in the past few years only on rare occasions, but now even this mild concession to the usual female grooming routine felt strange. As I carefully applied the lipstick one evening in preparation for a night out, it just didn't feel right any more. I was no longer trying to appear more feminine, and as the lipstick's job description was to achieve this, I realised it was time for us to finally go our separate ways. I still wanted to be well presented, and to look my best, but I was no longer trying to look particularly female. In fact, if I could begin looking more androgenous I would be happy.

Apart from a few fairly brief periods in my late teens and early twenties, when I sported long hair, I have always kept my wavy locks cut to varying degrees of short. If it had been at all socially acceptable I would have happily had it mere centimetres long all over. Now, I kept my hair as short as I dared. Luckily for me I think my style can handle leaning towards the minimalist look, as short hair actually suits me better than long. Now, each time my hair started to grow out to a more feminine length, I would begin to noticeably lose my confidence. Because I was now so emotionally male, the more female I looked, the more the disparity between what the world saw and what I felt inside, and the greater my discomfort level. It was a clear indication of just how completely I was now identifying emotionally as a man.

Although the world at large still saw me as a woman, I no longer identified myself as such in any way socially or emotionally at all. My pesky

X chromosomes and physical make-up were the only female aspects I had any attachment to and this was only due to necessity. Despite all of this, some of my attitudes hadn't, and wouldn't ever, change. I was still a feminist, deeply concerned about the many difficult and often dangerous issues women in Australia and across the world faced. Even though I had emotionally handed in my female membership badge I was still firmly holding onto my feminist one.

    In January 2015 I began my second attempt at writing a novel based on a transgender character. My fictional characters had been clamouring impatiently around inside my head before, during, and ever since I was in the U.K. and now I was finally allowing them to escape onto the page. My desire to add to the knowledge about the trans community was strong, and I believed that incorporating that information into an entertaining novel would be a good way to do it. A novel was safer than memoir as I didn't feel ready to "come out" and although some people would have their suspicions that the character was based on me, they wouldn't be sure. A novel gave me the freedom to decide if and when I would open wide that closet door and step through it. I certainly didn't feel anywhere near ready for that at the moment. After all, until a few years ago I didn't even realise that there was a closet for me to come out of.

    I enjoyed writing my novel, relishing the chance to use my imagination and simply make stuff up. It also meant my memory only had to break into the occasional sweat rather than be constantly forced into intensive work-outs, as it would have to if I was writing a memoir.

The result was, to put it mildly, unreadable. Apparently my skills as a novelist hadn't improved since my previous attempt, but I wasn't ready to admit defeat and decided to try again anyway. I was briefly tempted to write it as a true memoir, as I'd rather be telling my own story than that of a fictional character. But still being unwilling to come out, writing it as fiction was the only realistic option at this point.

I began my new storyline in October 2015, just a few days after relegating my previous attempt to the back of a desk drawer. I was hoping to have it completed by the end of 2016, just over a year away. This story, in one form or another, had been an itch in my psyche for years now, and I wouldn't be able to let it go until I turned it into a readable form.

2016 didn't begin well, with the shock death in January of one of my favourite performers, David Bowie. I admire him immensely, not only for his music but also because he had such a liberating effect on the cultural scene. Bowie didn't just colour outside the lines, he re-drew the lines. During his early career he was a major influence in helping to loosen the restrictive social constraints and attitudes of the times.

As often happens when an icon we have grown up with dies, there was a feeling that reality had shifted slightly. The world as we knew it had changed, and was a little emptier. I had no idea when I heard about the tragic passing of David Bowie that in a matter of months my family would be shattered by a loss much closer to home.

Progress was fairly slow on the novel as I was also attempting to cull my possessions ready to sell my house and downsize. The house was old and getting more crotchety and demanding by the year, with major repairs being urgently needed. As I didn't have the financial or motivational resources to give it the necessary attention, I decided it was time to move on.

But a few months before 2016 came to an end, both my writing and culling were put on hold when tragedy struck our family.

Chapter Twenty-Three

In August 2016 Sarah's husband Kevin died suddenly and unexpectedly from a massive heart attack, shortly after his 56th birthday. Even now as I write this two years later it still doesn't seem quite real that he is gone.

As Sarah said in her touching tribute to Kevin at his funeral, he was one of those rare people who was totally comfortable in their own skin. Kevin managed to fit more adventures and experiences into his fifty six years than many people do in eighty six, as well as positively touching the lives of so many on the way. He also left behind two daughters, Jasmine and Rebecca, beautiful young women that he had just had time to see grow into adulthood.

In the first few months after Kevin's passing my anxiety levels sky-rocketed. I was terrified that we could lose another member of the family at any time and for any, or no reason at all. It felt like Death was lurking in the shadows, perhaps ready to pounce again. Obviously I had always known the sudden death of a relative or close friend was possible, but until we lost Kevin I didn't really believe in the reality of it. It seems to be a natural and protective instinct that we can't quite believe such sudden tragedies could happen to us or those close to us. When it does, that protective veneer of self-delusion is stripped away and the world becomes a terrifying place as we fully realise the fragility of life.

    Our family were all still reeling from the shock and grief of Kevin's death when seven weeks later the nursing home rang. We were told that Dad had detiorated markedly, and that he probably only had days to live. He had been going steadily downhill for the past few weeks, so we weren't totally surprised by the news. We had been hoping that Dad's suffering would be over soon, but of course it was still terribly upsetting when it appeared that the end was finally nearing for him. We all immediately went to the nursing home to be with Dad, not knowing if he had hours or days left. It was a sunny day and we wheeled him outside into the gardens for what would be the last time. Shaun, Jasmine and Rebecca all said their goodbyes to their Granddad that day, and we hoped he knew they were there. I think he did.

    For the next three days Mum, Sarah and I spent each day at Dad's bedside. He couldn't move or speak but we felt that he was aware that we were there and could hear us talking to him. Justin, who was still in Ireland, was able to say his goodbyes through a Skype connection Sarah organised. Other family members also came for final, emotion-filled visits. Those last three days with Dad were incredibly painful, while simultaneously profound. As Sarah described it, it felt like a sacred experience being with him and offering comfort as he slowly slipped away. As Dad lay there fighting to breathe, it was as if he had been stripped down to his pure essence, with his soul all that was left. He looked so vulnerable that we felt as protective of him as if he was a newborn child.

Sometime in his final few months Dad had mentioned how pleased he was that he had achieved his early ambition to learn to fly. Although he had to give it up before actually gaining his pilot's license due to a virus causing hearing loss in one ear, he flew solo a number of times. I am so glad that Dad could remember this achievement as it was obviously a big comfort to him. And I hope he remembered that he had also achieved another of his major dreams, to create a productive wheat farm out of virgin bushland.

Dad loved language, and had a talent for penning poetry and short stories. He had a very good sense of humour, with some of his pieces being laugh-out-loud funny. At other times he would pen something profound or touching. Unfortunately he couldn't make the most of his writing talent as he didn't have the confidence to try writing a book, even though I think he would have liked to. Over the years Sarah has had several books published which have been very well received. So I like to think that even though Dad never wrote his own book, he played an important part in Sarah and I writing ours, by having passed his love of language onto us. He also, as did Mum, always encouraged us in our writing efforts, which we much appreciated.

Here is a short piece of Dad's writing which we found in his desk. I like to imagine that he wrote this in a spontaneous burst of creativity after coming in from his beloved garden one day.

"It was such a special, beautiful day, that the souls of the flowers, no longer able to remain earthbound, chased and pirouetted in the sky in the form of butterflies."

A. Barrett

Chapter Twenty-Four

In March 2017 I sold my house and bought a one bedroom apartment in a seaside suburb. Shaun, who had been living at home with me, moved into a small self-contained unit behind Mum's house. Although we had both appreciated the size of our old house we were glad to leave its ever-increasing maintenance demands and unruly garden behind.

I had been culling my possessions for quite awhile ready for down-sizing, but once I moved into my new and relatively tiny space I realised I would have to be more ruthless. My possessions would now have to meet an even higher standard to retain their right to residence. Paring down my possessions to the minimum caused two very conflicting emotions, which often appeared simultaneously. One was the sense of freedom that getting rid of non-essential stuff gave me. As another bag or box of evicted items left the apartment I felt a little less weight bearing down on me emotionally. On the other hand, each eviction notice was accompanied by the fear that I would regret the decision later. Especially anything that had even the slightest whiff of nostalgia coming off it.

Getting rid of anything I didn't need for practical or emotional purposes and streamlining my material possessions was like metaphorically pushing a re-set button. I was jettisoning the clutter and hopefully moving onto the next stage of my life with less physical baggage to weigh me down.

    I resumed writing my novel in June 2017, when I was partially settled into my new apartment. It had been almost a year since I had last looked at it. It was great to be working on it again, and although it was challenging writing about trans issues, as always I found the creative process therapeutic. I enjoyed being able to let my imagination loose to create a fictional world. A world where I was in control of the events that happened to my characters, rather than the frightening unpredictability of the real thing. But as I got further into it I started second-guessing myself, wondering if it would in fact be better as a true memoir. I would be sorry to have to abandon my main character, as it was fun living in her world rather than my own as I wrote, but I couldn't let that influence my decision.

    It wasn't long before I decided I would finally try writing about my own experiences, rather than recounting the imaginary life of an imaginary character. I think the loss of Dad and Kevin was a major influence in this final decision to write a true memoir. I now feel an almost overwhelming urgency to live life to the fullest while I have the chance, although I'm not yet sure exactly what form that will take. Dad sometimes used to remark, probably when someone had died, that "We're all just pencilled in." Now I'm very mindful of the

Universe's eraser that could be wielded at any time. Suddenly those pencil marks look more vulnerable than ever.

So the first major step in my efforts to live life to the full extent of my capabilities is to reveal my true story rather than hide it inside the fictional world of a novel. Hopefully, if my readers know that what they are reading is someone's real-life experience it will make the story more emotionally powerful and more satisfying for them. If I made it into a novel the blurred lines between fiction and facts would, I suspect, dilute its effect. Because my main reason for writing this book is to show one trans person's experience, making it about real life would presumably be a more effective way of achieving this.

Of course, this story is only intended to describe my own transgender journey and emotional experiences. Just like any group who have an issue in common, trans people all have their own personal and individual as well as some shared experiences. No two stories could ever be the same, just as no two cancer survivors, new parents, Academy Award winners, or anyone else's stories would be.

Also, the fact that I hadn't realised I was actually transgender until well into my forties might sound a bit far-fetched in a novel. Readers may feel that I was stretching the bounds of credibility in order to create a story. However, as the saying goes, truth is often stranger than fiction, and so, ironically, becomes believable if the reader knows it did actually happen that way.

    The prospect of outing myself was still rather terrifying, but I now felt more prepared to deal with it when the time came.

Chapter Twenty-Five

My transgender issues are growing increasingly restless. Although I'm not sure what I will have to do to appease them, I'm hoping that writing this memoir and tumbling out of the closet will be a positive first step.

Sarah's unwavering support and encouragement during my journey of self-discovery has been invaluable in helping me to reach this point, and is much appreciated. As Sarah said when I first realised who I am, I have finally identified my tribe. Now I have an increasing need to actually make contact with that tribe, rather than simply be an interested by-stander. I am still daunted by the prospect, but feel that it is time to explore the world outside the cramped confines of the closet. After all, in the past, some of my biggest adventures have happened when I've taken a huge step outside my dis-comfort zone.

Acknowledgements

This book owes its existence to the generous support and efforts of some wonderful people who helped me forge the unwieldy early drafts into a coherent shape.

My heartfelt thanks go to:

Sarah, for encouraging me to write my own true story rather than making it into fiction. Thank you too, for your multiple readings and perceptive editorial suggestions throughout the whole process. I am deeply appreciative of your considerable efforts and impressive editorial skills. You helped me forge a clear path through the tangled linguistic foliage of the numerous earlier drafts.

Mum, for your discerning and skilful editorial feedback, and your continual support of a manuscript which must have initially been very emotionally confronting.

Shaun, for your incisive editorial contributions, and your invaluable help with the composition and photography of the cover.

Jasmine, for reading pivotal parts of the manuscript and providing me with insightful, and also encouraging feedback.

Brett, for being my first reader outside

the family, and providing me with observant feedback on story structure. Your perceptive suggestions have made it stronger. Thank you too, for your unquestioning acceptance of my real identity.

Ziggy, for playing your guitar.

I also want to say a huge thank you to each of my family members who currently know about my transgender identity. You have all been unconditionally accepting and supportive, and I deeply appreciate it. Without your support I would never have written this memoir, and in the process, come completely out of the closet.

CPSIA information can be obtained
at www.ICGtesting.com
Printed in the USA
BVHW092134030119
536778BV00015B/591/P